Blueprint for a

GW01081384

GEORGE F

George Frankl was born in Vienna where he studied philosophy and psychoanalysis. The Nazi invasion of Austria forced him to emigrate and he eventually settled in London where he has been in psychoanalytic practice for over forty years. His work as a psychotherapist has attracted many followers, who consider his techniques to be a major breakthrough in the improvement of psychoanalytic treatment as well as in our understanding of the unconscious.

He has lectured on psychoanalysis, philosophy, prehistoric cultures and architectural psychology at several universities, and among his books, *The Failure of the Sexual Revolution* and *The Unknown Self* have been particularly widely acclaimed, both here and in the USA. But while actively engaged in writing, lecturing and his work as a psychotherapist, he was concerned with the social neurosis and determined to find an explanation for the compulsions which drive nations to pursue irrational and all too frequently self-destructive goals. He is now convinced that the most important achievement of psychoanalysis will emerge in its application to the social pathologies.

George Frankl's books have been translated into several languages.

'The Frankl school redefines libido – the primal drive of
the infant – not, as in Freud, as a sexual impulse but as an innate
need for love ... Frankl holds that our loving instincts turn into
aggression and destructive drives, if thwarted. The task is
to discover ... how primary love was turned into aggression; and then
he [Frankl] attempts to liberate not the aggression, but the love.
Frankl has, however, also evolved analytical strategies to cope with
the psychic dimensions of social behaviour.'

Prof. Erich Segal, *The Times Literary Supplement*

OTHER BOOKS BY GEORGE FRANKL

The End of War or the End of Mankind

The Failure of the Sexual Revolution

The Social History of the Unconscious

Archaeology of the Mind

Civilisation: Utopia and Tragedy

The Unknown Self

Exploring the Unconscious

Foundations of Morality

Blueprint
for a Sane Society

George Frankl

OPEN GATE PRESS

incorporating Centaur Press

LONDON

First published in 2004 by Open Gate Press
51 Achilles Road, London NW6 1DZ

British Library Cataloguing-in-Publication Programme
A catalogue record for this book is available from the British Library.

ISBN 1 871871 60 3

The author gratefully acknowledges permission to reproduce copyright material from:

The Times, on pp. 49–50, 62, 62–63, 107, 123–124 and 153–156. © Times Newspapers Limited.
The Sunday Telegraph, on p. 117;
The Guardian and Jeremy Seabrook, on p. 115;
The Evening Standard, on pp. 58, 104, 129–130;
The Ecologist, on pp. 137, 141–142, 144–147;
New Society (now part of *New Statesman*), on p. 99;
Prospect, on pp. 99–100.

The author would also like to thank Mrs Catherine M. Castree and Mr Julian Oxley for permission to reproduce material from their letters of 28th March 2002, to *The Times*, on p. 63.

Printed in Great Britain by Bell & Bain Ltd., Glasgow.

Contents

PART 2 *Practical*

CONTENTS

Why I became a Psychoanalyst

This book is in many respects the culmination of my work as a psychoanalyst. For more than forty years of therapeutic practice I have been engaged in exploring the mostly unconscious motivations which produce neurotic as well as psychotic disturbances, and have developed techniques which go beyond the cumbersome and unpredictable methods of free association and interpretation, to gain direct access to the unconscious areas of the mind and improve the prospects of cure.

What is most interesting and rewarding in psychoanalysis is that an understanding both by the therapist as well as the patient of the previously hidden processes of the mind, the exploration and re-experience of the traumas which were responsible for mental disturbances, makes it possible for the patients to relinquish their symptoms and regain a state of health. The thought that the new insights into the unconscious mind could be applied to the neurotic and even psychotic pathologies of societies was never far from my mind.

Even as a boy I was nonplussed by the illogical and irrational prejudices of grown-ups expressed with an air of self-righteous certitude, and it was not long before I became aware of political and religious ideas which I thought to be quite mad. In particular the propaganda of the Nazis, culminating in their take-over of Germany and eventually of Austria and their unspeakable brutalities shocked and disturbed me profoundly. But it was the perversity of the mind of those who justified them which outraged my way of thinking. Even before the onslaught of Nazism the arguments which maintained that wars are inevitable or even necessary made me wonder what makes people think like that. Most people of our acquaintance, friends of my father, many of them fellow soldiers of the First World War, passionately deplored warfare and turned against the propaganda which justified it. They became socialists, hoping that a socialist transformation of society would eliminate warfare and bring about a decent and peaceful social order. But very soon the debate between those who believed in the revolutionary transfer of power from capitalism to socialism through the dictatorship of the working class and those who believed in democratic reform – the debate between communism and social democracy – acquired a central position in post-war politics.

I remember my father deeply mistrusting the authoritarian dictatorship of the communist movement and passionately defending the democratic qualities of socialism. He often said that ends do not justify means, because the means adopted by a political movement will be reproduced by its regime once it gains power; that a violent and ruthless revolution would produce a violent and ruthless dictatorship, and the dictatorship of the proletariat would end up as a dictatorship over the proletariat. My mother, on the other hand, being a more down-to-earth person, argued that the bourgeoisie would not willingly acquiesce to the expropriation of its wealth and its privileges and would put up a fight to prevent it and produce a counter-revolution.

I heard these arguments as a little boy and they lived on in my mind. I sided with my father, for it seemed obvious to me that a socialism based on coercion would inevitably come to oppress people and defeat their aspirations for freedom and equality. On the other hand, my mother was also right in predicting the counterattack of the established upper and middle classes by means of a counter-revolution which soon took the form of Fascism and Nazism on the one hand, and a Stalinist feudal dictatorship[1] on the other. It was the battle between the two dictatorships Nazism and Communism, the two perversions of capitalism and socialism, which dominated the political life of Europe and turned a large part of the twentieth century into a nightmare. While Nazism was decisively defeated thanks to the heroic efforts of the nations who resisted the most cruel dictatorship of human history, Stalinism lived on for another forty years and not only continued to oppress, torture and kill people in the name of the people it claimed to represent, but also tortured the minds of intellectuals across the world. It too was defeated, not so much by war but by the outrage of its citizens over the incompetence and corruption of its centralised bureaucracy and economy which had impoverished the country.

But long before the collapse of Stalinist Communism, I could not countenance the notion of an oppressive dictatorship claiming to be the embodiment and realisation of the socialist dream. The liberation of the poor and the oppressed masses surely meant granting them freedom and a fair share of the wealth which they had produced by their labour, and affirming their personal dignity. No amount of political and ideological propaganda would deceive me in face of the blatant lies which attempted to hide the reality of their oppressive regimes. I became irritated and baffled by what appeared to be silly and dishonest arguments upholding inhuman political or religious convictions – the Catholic church was an outspoken supporter of the economic and political privileges of the traditional ruling class and a ruthless opponent of socialist reform – and I could not accept the dogma of mankind's fundamental sinfulness which I felt as a personal insult. I wanted to find out what makes people uphold views which were obviously stupid and nasty.

I decided to become a philosopher in order to understand the way the mind works, how it can produce visions of peace and freedom and at the same time justify the most atrocious acts of barbarism and cruelty. I read *The Communist Manifesto* and the writings of Otto Bauer and Viktor Adler, the ideological spokesmen of the Austrian Socialist Party committed to the abolition of injustice and poverty and the creation of a just society.

I then began to study the writings of the great philosophers, Plato, Kant and Schopenhauer, and expressed my enthusiasm for philosophy to my father and his friends: if only people would learn to think rationally, if they could cease to be dominated by prejudice, superstition and ignorance, a better world could be built. Kant in particular became my hero, and while it was often difficult to understand his writings, I recognised the profundity and revolutionary aspects of his thinking. I remember sitting in the park with Kant's *Critique of Pure Reason*, reading paragraph by paragraph and sometimes sentence by sentence, determined to understand what he really means behind the often obtuse propositions which to the normal habits of our thinking appeared very strange. In my mind I talked to him as person to person, and forced him to explain himself, which he seemed to do by making me read on and carefully analyse his sentences. I was not going to just repeat or memorise what he said, I wanted to understand his arguments before I could accept them. I was about thirteen years old at the time, and I am still grateful about my perseverance in my encounter with Kant, forcing him to make me understand by adopting a critical attitude to his great 'critiques'.

I remember at that time an occasion when I spoke to my father and his friends about the wonders of philosophy, and while they sympathised with my ideals, they pointed out that it is all very well for young people to entertain great romantic ideas, but as I grew up I would learn to be more realistic. I asked them whether they considered themselves to be realistic, and they said 'Yes, of course!' But I wanted to know whether they thought that poverty and wars are inevitable, whether accepting injustice and oppression, ignorance and prejudice, which cause so much misery, is being realistic. They had the decency to look embarrassed, and I could see that it made them think. I was pleased that upon reflection they agreed with me, and it confirmed my feelings that one has to speak up if one is confronted by silly ideas and speak one's mind.

My father who was a socialist even while he was a business man, sensitive to injustice and an idealist to the extent that he wanted to see a world without war and with respect for individuals of all classes, at the same time emphasised the need to be practical. While he clearly sympathised with my ideas, he thought that as a philosopher I would live in a sort of airy-fairy world with great ideas without being able to do anything practical about them. I found it, however, self-evident that one has to do something to promote people's rational faculties, to help them think clearly and encourage what Kant called 'the Good Will'. But above all I wanted to know what it is in the mind that impels otherwise decent people to accept the lunacy which overtakes nations as an inevitable fact of life.

At that time my father was a friend of Alfred Adler. They belonged to the same branch of the socialist party in the district of Vienna where we lived. Adler became a prominent adviser to the Ministry of Education which was committed to the transformation of education and schools. There was a widespread discussion whether the socialists should adopt Freudian ideas and make teachers of kindergartens and primary schools receive some psychoanalytic training. But this seemed far too complicated, and it was decided that Adlerian methods would be more practical for the purpose of raising the intellectual level of children and enabling them to become responsible and active members of the community. Adler agreed with Nietzsche's declaration that every human being should have a sense of his own power, not over others but as a creative or, as Kant had put it, a 'causative agent' in the making of a good society. I heard these arguments in the early Thirties and experienced many aspects of Adler's contribution in my early school days, when each child was given responsibility and some special task in organising the class-room and was encouraged to add up the oral and written examination results on the blackboard together with the teacher, to determine the grade which the pupil was to be given. By that time Adler had gone to America, where his lectures and teachings were widely acclaimed, but whenever he came back to Vienna he came to visit my father.

No doubt father told him about my aspirations in philosophy and my interest in the mind, and he talked to me about psychoanalysis and the unconscious, his concepts of a person's own power, and the community spirit. I eagerly took up the concept of the unconscious, which determines not only people's character but also their judgements, their ideas and beliefs. It became clear to me that if one wants to be a good philosopher one has to take the unconscious into account. But then I began to read Freud's writings, which I thought to be more thoroughgoing and profound than Adler's, and I resolved to become a psychoanalyst. My father was relieved at my new choice of profession, because it was something specific and practical I could do. My mother was pleased because she did not have a very high opinion of book learning alone without contributing in a tangible way to people's needs. I became convinced that theory and practice must go together, and in my eventual work as a psychoanalyst I have always endeavoured to apply theoretical understanding of the nature of neurotic determinants to the improvement of psychoanalytic technique, to be a theoretician as well as a craftsman. And then I became convinced that psychoanalysis, dealing with the psyche of individuals, should also be applied to the collective psyche of societies.

Shortly after the German invasion of Austria, my father was arrested and taken to Buchenwald. I eventually managed to emigrate to England, where I was able to obtain a permit for my parents to come as well. On the strength of it my father was released from the concentration camp, but it was too late, and I never saw him again. I was in England when he came out of Buchenwald, and my parents had to wait a few more weeks before they could come over. He told my young brother: 'Tell George that he must explain how such terrible things can happen.' My brother left Vienna on the day war broke out and managed to come to England. My parents were not long afterwards arrested and taken to Theresienstadt concentration camp and then deported to Auschwitz where they were killed. I resolved to fulfil my father's plea.

Eventually I applied Freud's discoveries about the unconscious processes of the mind to the evolution of cultures from earliest times, but I had to revise some of his ideas which were stuck in a patriarchal mould, as he could not have been aware of the important archaeological discoveries of man's prehistory which were made after his death. Just as the experiences of earliest childhood have a powerful influence upon a person's character, so the events of man's prehistory have a significant influence upon subsequent cultures up to the present. This seemed to me quite self-evident, if one takes an evolutionary view of life, and psychoanalysis is nothing if not evolutionary, phylogeny and ontogeny being complementary to each other. One may call the earliest experiences of a person which are subsequently forgotten the unconscious part of his mind – his prehistory, and his conscious self, his memories of childhood and adolescence – his history. Equally, the collective mind of a culture as it is reproduced in the mind of its members and transmitted by narratives, myths, traditions and rituals, can be called its history.

I wrote a book on the social history of the unconscious in two parts: Prehistory: *Archaeology of the Mind*, and History: *Civilisation: Utopia and Tragedy*. After many years as a therapist and learning from my patients' experiences of the unconscious areas of the mind, as well as from current archaeological research and social anthropology, I wrote *The Unknown Self*, a book on the psychological development of the individual – from his experiences during infancy to his relationship to the world as a grown-up – and on the unconscious motivations of civilisations and politics.

I was then persuaded to give an account of the therapeutic techniques and methods which I had developed over the years. *Exploring the Unconscious* is essentially a practical guide to a new method of therapy I have developed which enables patients not only to remember but to re-experience their early infantile as well as adolescent traumas and opens the door to the hidden world of the unconscious areas of the mind. This therapeutic technique, which employs some hypnosis, shows a dramatic improvement in the success rate of psychoanalysis compared with its traditional method of free association and interpretation.

For some time now it has been common to speak of psychoanalysis as a discipline in crisis. Cecilio Paniagua argues that "any psychoanalytic interpretation which is so below the conscious 'surface' that it cannot be verified by the patient's own capacities, is suggestion," and raises the question on what basis we can argue that "our daily psychoanalytic work does capture demonstrable unconscious phantasies that belong to the patient rather than the analyst" (*The International Journal of Psychoanalysis*, August 2001).[2] In my own work I always attempt to make quite sure that the patient not only re-experiences the emotional traumas which have previously been repressed and forgotten, but also understands how they have produced his symptoms and personality problems.

But then I turned again to the cultural problems and conflicts of our civilisation. In my recent book *Foundations of Morality*, I show that moral concepts are necessary in human beings and how they developed in the evolution of our species. I describe the breakdown of moral values in our time, the erosion of religious beliefs with the spread of the Enlightenment, and how, in turn, the Enlightenment has failed to fulfil the hopes and expectations of a rational and peaceful world order, leaving people disenchanted and increasingly cynical, unable to believe in anything but immediate, short-term gratification. This has made it difficult to sublimate primitive drives into civilised values which we can no longer believe in. I look at the explosion of crime and violence, particularly among the young, who break the laws and outrage traditional norms of behaviour without remorse or any sense of guilt. On the other side of the social spectrum we find an obsession with profit and money-making among the commercial and financial corporations, whose shareholders, chairmen, directors and dealers seem unconcerned about the damage they do to the natural environment. In their relentless pursuit of self-enrichment they impoverish the earth and arouse the envy and hostility of the underdeveloped nations.

It was to be expected that philosophers – determined to be up to date and scientific – joined the fashion for debunking moral aspirations and justified the moral vacuum by convoluted arguments in the name of rationalism. They set out to prove that all metaphysics, which includes moral concepts, is 'non-sense'. Logical positivists, linguistic analysts and deconstructionists combined to prove that ideas not based upon the evidence of the senses are an illusion – beyond the perception of what is the case – and are to be dismissed by philosophy.

However, recent discoveries by neurologists and the new brain sciences have shown that there is a built-in structure in the human brain which operates the intellectual processes such as foresight and anticipation beyond 'what is the case', and above all the area of the cortex which is the seat of morality – the moral neurons, as they are called – which has to be exercised in order to fulfil the potential of the human mind. It has taken a million years to develop and has made us different from all other animals. Its neglect has a catastrophic effect upon the intellect and the psyche of individuals and cultures. What Theodor Adorno has called the stupefication process of late capitalism or, as it is nowadays termed, the 'dumbing down' process, which we can see in the arts, in literature, theatre and the media which feed us with violence and brutality and by defying civilised values encourage destructive and self-destructive compulsions, can now be explained in a scientific manner.

Having examined the neurological foundations of moral concepts and how they have developed, I set out to show how they can be brought back to life and proposed a set of moral imperatives, taking my cue from Kant, to provide new directions for our behaviour. I consider these imperatives and maxims to be convincing and life affirming, but while it is relatively easy to develop abstract ideas and principles of how we ought to think and behave, it is very difficult to apply them in practice in a world riddled with a multitude of prejudices and unexamined goals.

I therefore decided without further ado to make a blueprint for a sane society to prevent the blind rush towards self-extermination.

The evidence of history and of our own time makes it obvious that mankind periodically falls victim to a disease of the mind which can devastate cities and destroy civilisations, killing millions of people. But now the disease has the means at its disposal to threaten the survival of humanity and life on this planet. This nightmare scenario has brought home to us that the danger is very real now, due to the nuclear and biochemical weaponry available to religious fanatics who in the name of their god intend to destroy Western civilisation and kill anyone who does not share their religious beliefs. The question which confronts us is whether the disease is terminal and incurable or whether it can be cured, whether it is a manifestation of a collective psychosis which is impervious to reason and argument or whether it is a kind of neurosis which is open to treatment – the difference between insanity and a neurotic disturbance of our mental faculties as exemplified by the aberrations of Western civilisation which we can hope to cure. If the latter is the case, then a project for the rehabilitation of human sanity must be justified, and the urgency of such a project must be obvious.

When I began writing this book, I meant to apply my analysis to the collective pathology of Western society without much reference to cultures outside our own. September 11th 2001 shocked me and everybody else into recognising a pathology, a kind of madness which suddenly erupted into the Western world, when the barbarism of the Middle Ages with its religious fanaticism invaded our own time. The pathologies of the West are small fry compared to the brutalities of the Muslim fanatics, and I am now obliged to take them into account if I am to do some justice to my quest for social sanity.

PART 1 Theoretical

CHAPTER 1

What is Sanity?

The diagnosis of collective neuroses will be confronted by a special difficulty. In the neurosis of an individual we can use as a starting-point the contrast presented to us between the patient and his environment which we assume to be 'normal'. No such background as this would be available for any society similarly affected; it would have to be supplied in some other way. And with regard to any therapeutic application of our knowledge, what would be the use of the most acute analysis of social neuroses, since no one possesses the power to compel the community to adopt the therapy? In spite of all these difficulties, we may expect that one day someone will venture upon this research into the pathology of civilized communities.

Sigmund Freud: *Civilization and Its Discontents*

When we speak of health (*sanitas*), we assume that the organic processes of the body such as metabolism, hormones, the respiratory, circulatory, digestive and nervous systems function satisfactorily and contribute without impediment to its growth and well-being. Healthy people can pursue their chosen activities without experiencing pain, shortage of breath or undue exhaustion; their appetite is good and they enjoy their food and digest it without trouble; their muscular system enables them to carry out the necessary tasks of moving, working, walking, running and enjoying sporting activities; the heart operates well and fulfils its task of pumping blood and oxygen to the brain and bodily organs, and their genital organs react vigorously to their sexual urges and desires and if aroused respond with elation, expansion and orgastic discharge. In other words, people can be pleased and proud of their body and enjoy its exercise.

When we speak of a healthy mind we assume that it promotes

3

a person's sense of well-being, co-ordinating the multiplicity of his drives and desires into a unified and fairly harmonious sense of self and satisfies his self-image. In the same way as a person's body separates him from other persons and acquires its own identity but needs others to satisfy its needs for nourishment, shelter, clothing and security, the mind of a person is unique to himself and separates him from others but needs their attention, their responsiveness and acknowledgement and their support, as they are reference points for his self-esteem by which he judges himself.

A person's mind which is able to successfully sublimate primitive, infantile and anti-social impulses into socially acceptable pursuits and transform the chaotic impulse-dominated demands of the id into a conscious self-image which he can like and respect, is considered a healthy mind. If he can in some measure love and respect himself, he can also show love for others and will respond to their needs to be loved and to be understood and respected. This is the foundation of empathy with his fellow-men, and also with the life of nature, which is seen not merely as a means, as an object to be used and exploited; he is aware of the needs of his environment, both human as well as natural, and is able to adapt and modify his expectations and behaviour accordingly. Beyond the consideration of his own personal interests he will be aware of the interests of others, as he wants to be accepted and valued by them. He will recognise impulses and desires which damage his relationships or offend the rules of behaviour adopted by society. He will encourage and enjoy effort-making to fulfil tasks and goals which he sets himself, and feel a sense of satisfaction and gratification if his efforts are recognised and appreciated by his fellow-men.

A person may feel that the values of society are immoral and irrational and will uphold alternative values which seem to him to be right and which at the same time he can examine by the exercise of his rational faculties. If, however, he refuses to question or examine his motivations and the validity of his convictions and considers anybody who disagrees with him his enemy, then we can speak of him as a possibly dangerous fanatic and in varying degrees mentally disturbed. We find a wide range of such fanatics who refuse to examine the harm they cause, entrenched as they are in their obsessive pursuits. There are, however, many individuals who are subject to anxieties and obsessions, who, despite their awareness that their fantasies, fears and rages are unrealistic and contrary to their real inclinations, nevertheless are not able to control them. We speak of such people as being neurotic.

Neurotic Symptoms.

These include chronic anxiety, phobias, manic-depressive cycles with paranoic fantasies; chronic jealousy and envy; obsessions and compulsions; disturbing feelings of guilt and a sense of worthlessness; difficulty in relating to people; uncontrolled rebellion against cultural standards and rules; powerful aggressive drives; sadistic as well as masochistic urges; a compulsion to defy rules and traditions; fear of flying or of falling, of being in a moving vehicle, such as a motor car or train; a sense of immobility and chronic tiredness. Fear of sexuality – frightened of women, frightened of men, general hatred of the other sex; obsession with hiding oneself in secretiveness; inability to enter into a discussion without anxiety or even panic. Fear of darkness and fear of light; agoraphobia or claustrophobia; conflicts between assertiveness and exaggerated submissiveness; apologetic behaviour and excessive self-doubt.

These are some of the most prevalent symptoms, but what they have in common is an awareness in the person suffering from them that they are neurotic, that the obsessions which dominate their minds or their behavioural compulsions, however painful and debilitating, are manifestations of a neurosis. For instance, one patient, a brilliant academic and lecturer, after a particularly good lecture and receiving the approval and admiration of his audience, was overwhelmed by panic feelings that he had said the wrong things and that people would criticise and attack him. Another patient, a professor of philosophy who had received international acclaim and was proud of it, nevertheless was overwhelmed by the feeling that he does not really exist.

5

Only a part of their mind is affected by an unknown force over which they have no control but know to be unrealistic and unreasonable.

Psychotic Symptoms.

Individuals who have lost their sense of reality and whose ego is swamped by infantile drives and fantasies, which in a normal person would be controlled and repressed to become unconscious, have lost their defence mechanisms and are classified as psychotic. They maintain that their fantasies are completely realistic and that other people who do not believe in their images and their judgements are completely wrong. They may hear a voice from heaven – of a god or a devil – whose commandments they have to obey, or think that they are all-powerful or that they are punished by the world and tortured or that water and food or air are poisoned and threaten to kill them.

The most common forms of insanity are classified as mania ('folie grandeur', as it was aptly called), often alternating with deep depression and a sense of utter worthlessness; dementia, paranoia ('paranoia major', as it was called), obsessive and unrealistic fears of being persecuted and attacked, catatonic immobility of mind and body, compulsions to carry out certain actions either of a reflex type of bodily movements or ritualistic repetitiveness, sadistic, destructive or masochistic self-destructive compulsions. Destructive and suicidal compulsions can overtake religious fanatics who believe that by their suicidal self-sacrifice they are liberated from their sense of worthlessness in the world and are assured of a heavenly paradise. Their ego – the sense of self – having been deprived of its narcissistic needs by an indifferent or rejective environment, becomes helpless and empty and is inundated with infantile fears and phobic fantasies. Their instinct for self-preservation gives way to a destructive rage, either against themselves or the world around them, and being unable to deal with the real world they shut it out from their mind, and their obsessive fantasies take the place of reality. They abdicate all sense of responsibility for what they do to others and obliterate moral considerations. But as we have seen, such processes can also overwhelm the collective psyche of nations and religious cultures.

The Difference between the Collective Neuroses and Psychoses of Society.

While I have drawn attention to the differences between neurotic and psychotic pathologies in individuals, we also have to distinguish between neurotic and psychotic disturbances of societies.

A society can be considered neurotic if its members can recognise various aspects of a malaise which has befallen their nation and are able to discuss and express opinions about its causes and what could be done to change and improve things. Despite the turmoil, the confusions and conflicts which they encounter, people still uphold the basic principles of the Enlightenment which emphasised men's rights and the duty to think for themselves, to examine the values and aims of their society and make their criticisms heard, and to express their opinions accordingly: 'Dare to think and cultivate your rational faculties in order to judge between right and wrong'. Thus the civilisations of the West still uphold the fundamental rules of democracy which they have inherited from the Enlightenment and are inscribed in the 'Rights of Man'.

However, in what I call 'psychotic cultures' there is no possibility for change or argument, for criticism and freedom of self-expression. In these cultures men have to submit to the commands of their religion which represent the will of God, who is eternal, omniscient and unchangeable and demands unquestioning submission to his commands, even if it means killing as many enemies as possible in wars or acts of terrorism.

The Koran, held to be the revealed word of God, describes Allah in all its supplications as all-merciful and all-compassionate and yet sees him as an avenging God exercising stern retribution upon those who do not submit to him. It proclaims *jihad* a duty for all the faithful of Islam: it is a command 1) to conquer the vices and passions in the mind of its followers;

7

2) to spread the word of Islam and convert the unbelievers by means of the tongue; 3) to do good and in practice carry out Allah's command by means of the hand and serve Islam and obey its rulers; 4) to conquer and defeat those who do not submit to Allah by the sword.

Muslims who consider themselves to be moderate will concentrate upon the first three rules of the *jihad*, but in the last resort, when persuasion and propaganda fail, when diplomacy and politics are unable to further the aims of Islam, it is the ultimate duty of the faithful to join the call to the sword, to fight against the infidel. Those who give up their lives either in battle or in suicidal missions will be rewarded with admission to an eternal paradise. Even the moderate Muslims will identify with their heroes in their ultimate act of Islamic virtue.

Western civilisation, which is committed to a respect for life and considers the instinct of self-preservation to be self-evident, reacts with particular horror to a deliberate act of suicide aimed at killing as many enemies, civilians, innocent bystanders, men, women and children as possible, and views the leaders of the *jihad* who persuade young men to kill themselves by making fanciful promises that they will enter paradise and have seventy virgins at their service to provide them with a life of infinite pleasures, as the representatives of ultimate cruelty and barbarism.

But, it may be asked, what right do we have to be surprised and horrified about such perversions of the human mind and to pontificate about human rights when we look at the atrocities and the barbarism which have overtaken Western civilisation in the twentieth century. Who can forget the horrors of two world wars, the murder of six million people in concentration camps, the obscene savagery of Nazism, and Stalinist communism which killed, starved and tortured some ten million people in the Gulags during a reign of terror in the name of socialism and poisoned the mind of many Western intellectuals who upheld the right of Stalinism to defend itself against the capitalist enemy. It is, however, true that the bastions of Western democracy together with the Soviet Union defeated Nazi Germany, and that eventually the people of the Soviet Union managed to rid themselves of their dictators. But still the hatred inspired by religious fanaticism has turned the Balkans into a battleground, and it needed the intervention of the democratic nations to bring some semblance of peace to the area and enable people of various religions to learn that they once again can live together without butchering each other.

So perhaps we have to admit, as many cynics tend to do, that the onslaught of barbarism from the East in the first year of the twenty-first century, however shocked and horrified we are, represents a deep-seated pathology of the human mind, which became genetically programmed during the evolution of our species and periodically overwhelms human beings with a kind of madness when reason and morality goes overboard and turns us into savages.

When, however, we speak of 'savages' we tend to refer to the behaviour and states of mind of our early ancestors which we thought we had overcome a long time ago. We refer to characteristics which early humans had acquired in the course of their evolution over a million years when what we call 'savagery' would have been considered quite normal; their brain had not yet developed the large frontal lobes of the brain of modern man which control the primitive drives and are the seat of our intellectual and moral capacity. But if we observe the behaviour of contemporary humans who are overwhelmed and dominated by the primitive drives, which are still stored in our brains, we refer to them as savages.

We do not need to go back to the long distant past to observe patterns of behaviour among African tribes for instance who regularly engage in tribal warfare, often of the most brutal and destructive kind even in our own time. While they have a brain not dissimilar to our own, they do not activate the prefrontal lobes in the way we do. Those parts of our brain which have the potential for empathy and respect for life have to be taught and activated. Our modern 'civilised culture' has implanted in our minds – with varying degrees of success – certain moral commandments, such as 'Love thy neighbour as thyself', 'Do not do to others what you do not want them to do to you', 'Thou shalt not kill'. These are moral rules pronounced as commandments by the Jewish prophets and by Rabbi Jesus, whose followers eventually started their own religion called Christianity which spread its message all over Europe and eventually America, and built the framework for what we call Western civilisation. African tribes did not acquire such moral commandments, they did not inherit the teachings of monotheism of the Jewish or Christian version, nor did they inherit the development of Greek philosophy, the Renaissance and the Enlightenment. Even nationhood, as we understand it, has not fully developed among them, and they periodically disrupt their newly acquired national establishments as their tribes continue to fight against each other for supremacy and power. It is a fact that even in our highly civilised way of life the old tribal rivalries break out in a sublimated but nevertheless equally ferocious manner in the form of business or national interests, turning nation states into killing machines.

Humans seem to have a profound difficulty overcoming the long acquired instinct to preserve and defend their tribal community against outsiders. For hundreds of thousands of years males had to fight against dangerous and powerful animals and kill them for food as vegetation became scarce during the Ice Ages and no longer provided sufficient nourishment, and our ancestors became killer apes.

The dualism between the world of the home – the cave, the family, the tribe, the community – and the world outside which had to be fought for sustenance and security, ensured that the imperative 'us against them' became gradually extended to 'my nation and other nations', 'my religion, my God' and 'alien religions and gods', and became deeply engrained in the human mind in a perennial splitting process. To defend one's own God, one's king, one's nation, against the 'others' who are seen as enemies, is upheld as a necessary and supreme duty. Even the three monotheistic religions which proclaim the existence of a God of the universe who created all life and all human beings upon whom he extends his special love as the crown of his creation – brothers and sisters united in his fatherhood, have not ceased to fight each other, and consider themselves rivals and enemies, proclaiming themselves to be the true followers of the Father's will and commandments.

But how is one to explain the confusions and discontents of our Western society, blessed by the unparalleled affluence of its free enterprise capitalist democracies? We can no longer recognise a clear pattern or cause for the apparently disconnected pathologies and miseries of modern life. It is true that there are many explanations, and I shall just mention a few: chemical fertilisers and pre-packaged meals containing a multitude of artificial preservatives; the restless hunger to acquire things to possess; greed and the cult of the acquisitive society; racism and the influx of foreign races and cultures which disturb the sense of identity and traditions of native citizens and create fear and resentment, and, at the same time, provoke aggressive reactions among the immigrant population, particularly among the young; the explosion of crime, drug addiction, robbery and increasingly violent attacks on innocent bystanders; the break-up of a feeling of community and a sense of belonging created by the bond of shared traditions, memories and values, making people feel increasingly estranged from each other and themselves. There is an increase in psychological disturbances, from neurotic symptoms for which the affluent can afford to receive treatment, to the psychiatric cases who fill mental hospitals and can be seen in abundance on the streets of towns and often show violent and psychopathic behaviour.

The Confusion of Western Civilisation.

Whereas 'in the old days' the impoverished and helpless working class was seen as the focal point of the crisis in Western society and found its Marxist explanation in the theory of the class war, proclaiming the revolutionary struggle against capitalism and the creation of the classless society the ultimate goal of history, the traditional working class is now diminished and is no longer recognised as the vanguard of revolutionary change. There is a demographic change in 'post-industrial' society where computer technology has transformed the modes of production and computer-controlled robotism dominates mass production. The traditional capitalist who owned the factories and was known by the workers, has been replaced by chairmen and directors of financial conglomerates, insurance companies, banks and their major shareholders whose function in running the factory is unclear. The 'worker by hand', identified by his manual skills, gives way to computerised machines, and the modern work-force takes its orders from them.

Not only a person's skill but also his intelligence is dependent upon his ability to absorb the information provided by the new technology; a person's skill is judged by his ability to absorb information presented by mathematical, statistical and quantitative codes which are seen as knowledge and widely regarded as the key to succeed in the world. A person's skill, his imagination and foresight in the production of commodities, is replaced by computers, the internet and websites, which require instant responses from the operator, quick push-button reactions which allow no time for thinking and the use of his own intellect about the state of the nation which is no longer his responsibility. His intellectual horizon has shrunk, while his reasoning processes are of a kind which Marcuse and Horkheimer called instrumental reasoning when his rational faculties are merely the means to further his self-interest and that of his employer in whatever career or way of life he is engaged in or aspires to.

Post-industrial capitalist enterprises dominated by information technology employ an increasing number of office workers, publicity consultants, sales managers, accountants, financial advisers as well as economists and scientists who have to use their reasoning abilities to accomplish the tasks set before them. They are specialists whose specialised horizons cannot cope with the increasing complexity of modern life, and they leave it to other specialists to look after the areas of life which they themselves are not competent to deal with and know little about. 'What I don't know, I don't need to know' has become a mindset even among the experts who have studied at universities and received degrees.

But the proliferation of skills required in modern society has forced a growing number of 'universities', and those which used to be polytechnics, to parade as universities even though they are no more than 'trade schools'. The word university is derived from *universitas*, meaning the teaching of universal knowledge as propagated by the Greeks, and particularly by Plato, and later by the mediaeval Christian monasteries teaching the knowledge of God, the creator of the universe. In the philosophy of Plato we discover the unity of man's innate reason, the Good and the Beautiful, while in God we partake in the unity of life, and our belief and worship gives meaning to our existence. The ancient universities of England, such as Oxford, don't seem to be quite sure whether they are modelled on Plato's Academy or the mediaeval monasteries.

Having lost the sense of unity both of the world and our knowledge of it in the increasing atomisation of learning into an infinite number of specialisms, we have become strangers to the areas of life outside our competence and beyond our responsibility: we are not responsible for what we don't know. We may be aware of many things which affect us in our lives, disturbing or pleasant, but we usually react to them emotionally without understanding, driven by our own psychological dispositions or by unexamined prejudices governed by religious or political indoctrination; we accept them in an uncritical manner and take them for granted as inevitable facts of life, and do not have a sense of our power to influence the world, to be active agents in the shaping of our destiny – it's all too complicated and there is nothing we can do about it.

If on the other hand people have strong convictions about some areas which are deemed wrong in our society, they are governed by their emotions, such as the rage which some people feel towards the fox-hunting fraternity or the passion for the protection of animals, when, in order to give vent to their feelings, they torture the horses of the fox-hunters and inflict the most cruel injuries upon them, like pushing a wooden pole up the vagina or the bottom of a horse (this is not hypothetical, it actually happened a number of times). Others choose to ignore the bloodshed and mass murder of the tribal wars in Africa, as for instance the war between the Hutus and Tutsis when something like two million were killed and the country was left desolate.

On the more civilised level we find the very fashionable and

13

dogmatic rule of 'political correctness' which is imposed upon Western people in the name of sexual, racial and cultural equality. It inflicts a censorship upon discrimination between the merits of different cultures and condemns admiration for the achievements of Western civilisation as cultural imperialism.

How many who pronounce the virtues and duties of political correctness realise that this phrase was first coined by Mussolini and enforced by Stalin and other dictators such as Saddam Hussein who could not tolerate differences of opinion among their people? Tolerance surely means acknowledging and respecting people's traditions and beliefs, as long as they don't harm others and wage wars against those who differ from them. Under the guise of tolerance the modern proselytes of human rights intimidate people and make them afraid to speak their minds and express their opinions; they put a taboo upon discrimination and value judgement, and one is no longer allowed to call a 'spade a spade' or use one's common sense. Do they realise that the censorship upon discrimination flaunts the basic rule of logic and contributes to the 'dumbing down' of the intellect and the exercise of one's rational faculties? Have they examined their reasons for setting themselves up as the dictators of tolerance? Have they asked themselves whether as members of the affluent middle class they feel superior to the 'ordinary' people of their own society and to other races and cultures, but patronise them by showing them their sympathy and goodwill?

They feel guilty about their sense of being superior, which they want to suppress by projecting it upon their fellow citizens, stirred by the collective memories of the British Empire which in their minds had oppressed the native races. They are determined to project their bad consciences upon their own society and Western civilisation as a whole, and force its members to make retribution for their misdeeds in the past by condemning any racial or sexual discrimination, and consider other races who live among them innocent of wrongdoing and victims of the white man's prejudices. If they commit a crime it must be considered the result of their sense of oppression and social exclusion. There is an epidemic of litigation by individuals who maintain they have been dismissed from jobs because of racial or sexual discrimination, where dispassionate and objective examination of such cases and the reasons for their dismissals tend to be ignored, and lawyers line their pockets by taking up the cause of political correctness. [1]

There is a widespread confusion, with conflicting opinions about whether governments should keep taxation as low as possible and let the well-to-do pay for private medical treatment and the school fees for the best education of their children. Should public transport be run by private companies or by the state? Should we encourage young people, even children, to believe that in the name of freedom it is their right to have sexual relationships before they are aware of the responsibilities involved? Should we respect our traditions or defy them?

And there is the confusion about the kind of entertainment people want and the freedom of the media, in particular television, to provide it. There are widespread complaints about the violent images and offensive language in popular programmes and their influence upon children. In one programme there was a scene in which a woman was tortured by having her head immersed in boiling fat.

While there was a 14% increase in sexual attacks across England and Wales and 27% in rapes during the last year, we are experiencing a dramatic increase in drug addiction and drug peddling by gangs, accompanied by gang warfare, and the involvement of children in terror attacks and shootings. Across England and Wales crimes of violence have increased by more than 20%, making many people apprehensive and insecure in their daily lives.

At the same time we are being assured by governments and their economists that living standards in Western society have risen and the quality of life has vastly improved. This is measured by the rise in consumption and the money available to the average citizens. So, what is one supposed to think?

These are but a few examples of the conflicts and confusions which beset the countries of the West, and we must ask how we can resolve them if we cannot think or imagine what a healthy and sane society should look like.

We are already in the process of damaging the biosphere

through our relentless exploitation of the natural resources in order to satisfy our apparently unstoppable hunger for more and more consumer goods, which is encouraged and abetted by our consumerist culture whose economy depends for its survival on the steady increase of the purchasing power of the public. The mass production of consumer goods pollutes the seas and the rivers with the refuse of industry and poisons the air; large-scale deforestation diminishes the oxygen in our atmosphere, causing the ozone layer (which made life as we know it possible on this planet) to shrink; the greenhouse effect and global warming, which is melting the ice of the polar regions, makes a rise in the ocean levels inevitable. This in turn causes a higher degree of evaporation and increases the rainfall, which again raises the water levels so that large, low-lying areas of the continents will be flooded and made uninhabitable.

At the same time we are producing nuclear and biochemical weapons of destruction, which harness the forces of cosmic energy, and the most primitive bacteria and viruses, which, if spread in high concentration, can poison and kill millions of people.

One can of course argue that if humankind destroys itself it is nothing very special or unique in the history of living organisms. Species come and go, they reach a certain stage of their evolution and then die out. We know of many examples, but there are probably thousands, if not millions, of species which have failed to cope with changes in their environment and, in the battle for survival of the fittest, had to make room for others to take up the challenge of preserving and developing life on earth. But the self-induced extermination of a species is of a completely new order.

'Homo sapiens', as we like to call ourselves, has in the course of evolution been endowed with the faculties of intelligence unique in the animal kingdom: his capacity of foresight and anticipation of the result of his actions, to plan ahead and to visualise in his mind optimum conditions for his survival, to choose between right and wrong, good and bad. We have developed the ability to transform the environment to serve our needs and to create conditions best suited for our survival and general well-being. Our species has acquired mastery over all other species and, to a great extent, over nature. The world in which we live is largely our own product, even though we are not aware that we have made it the way it is and then confront it as the reality to which we have to adjust. Mankind, therefore, is responsible for the damage it causes to the planet and its biosphere. If we use our intellectual endowment to destroy or poison our own species, we betray the rational and moral capacities which as a species we have acquired during our long evolution from unicellular organisms to the complex and wonderful nature of our brain and our mind which must be protected, and we have the innate capacity to do this. Those of us who love life and respect it cannot be indifferent to what we are doing to destroy it.

What are the Chances for a Therapy to Cure Mankind's Self-Destructive Compulsions?

Let us come back to our present reality and find out what we can do to avert the drift to catastrophe.

When a person comes to a therapist he will first of all present him with his symptoms, his conflicts and anxieties, his depressions or obsessions. With the help of the therapist he is led to discover what lies behind his symptoms and their causes, and hopes to acquire the ability to understand and to resolve them. Equally, if one wants to resolve the manifestations of a social neurosis or psychosis one has to be aware of the symptoms.

But it is not enough to be able to describe the symptoms – one has to understand their causes.

In his distinction between Eros and Thanatos, the love of life and the death drive as the two divine forces which constantly battle for dominance, Freud regarded them as two fundamental or eternal instincts battling for our soul. But while I agree that Eros, the love of life, is an instinct, I do not think that the death drive is an instinct, but a secondary drive generally caused by the denial of Eros, a desperation with life, a desire to escape from it, a drive to kill the self which cannot cope with the complexities and conflicts of its mind and wants to kill the world which is perceived as hostile and degrading. Thus it is a secondary drive even while it is very powerful. We therefore have to ask how the death drive in its manifestation of aggression and destruction arrived in the mind of mankind. Of course, one cannot psychoanalyse every individual on this planet, but one can psychoanalyse cultures.

The question which confronts us is why the aspirations for peace and justice are defeated with depressing regularity, why irrational compulsions frequently gain the upper hand, both in the life of individuals as well as societies. Mankind's aspirations for peace and justice are most certainly desirable and admirable, for they give expression to the potential of the human mind and are inscribed in his brain. Freedom, for instance, expresses the demands of the most advanced part of the cortex – the frontal lobes – which demands the freedom to make choices between possible actions; the idea of justice derives from our awareness of the harm we can do to others, as they can to us; and equality derives from the feeling of empathy with other humans.

But these areas of the brain can be put out of action or their functioning greatly reduced, either by an injury to the front of the brain but more frequently by cultures which promote the ancient and more primitive areas of brain – aggression, greed and the lust for power over others – while they discourage the exercise of the frontal lobes, the higher areas of the mind.

If we want to understand the causes of these conflicts we have to take an evolutionary view to find out how they developed, both in the life of individuals and also in societies; for the psyche of individuals and the psyche of cultures constantly interact. It has been said that the psyche of an individual is a small society and society a large individual. I have made a study of man's early evolution by applying a psychoanalytic anthropology in *The Social History of the Unconscious*. Here I want to go back to the earliest periods of a person's life and trace mankind's basic needs, not merely from birth but even – and this is certainly very surprising for it has never been properly considered before – from the embryonic stage.

CHAPTER 2

Mankind's Fundamental Needs

The Life of the Embryo.

There has been a upsurge of studies in the last twenty years which throw a new light upon the life of the embryo, about which hardly anything is known to the public.

Winnicott repeatedly emphasises that "if human babies are to develop eventually into healthy, independent and society-minded adults, they absolutely depend on being given a good start, and this good start is assured in nature by the existence of the bond between the baby's mother and the baby, the thing called love,"[1] and it starts before the infant is born, during the embryonic stage. "There is evidence that the foetus interacts with its environment," which is its mother, her womb, and it has been described as "a sentient, active organism capable of regulating and monitoring its environment."[2] "It is affected in a total psychosomatic way by its experience of its environment," i.e. the mother, and has the "means of recording it."[3] Fedor-Freybergh describes pregnancy as "an active dialogue between mother and child."[4] The mother communicates her emotions of love and happiness as well as her negative emotions, such as irritation with the encumbrance of pregnancy, resentment, or not having enough time to enjoy the prospect of having a child, being too busy and torn between the obligations of motherhood and being a working, wage-earning person.

The astounding discoveries of the active interaction between the foetus and mother, and the embryo's awareness of the mother's feelings and attitudes towards it, show the importance of the embryonic period for the formation of character, the health or the disturbances of the post-natal baby. While I have constantly emphasised the importance of the earliest experiences of the individual, even during the first hours and days of his life, we are discovering a new dimension of experience before the individual is born. The embryo is entirely immersed in the mother, it introjects – takes in – the mother's feeling and it feels with her, and the mother's mind becomes its own mind. Her love for the person inside her will make the embryo feel loved and loving, and her happiness will make it happy, and its experiences of empathy will make it capable of empathy. One can say that its perception of the mother is not based upon the sense organs which develop later, but upon the periphery of its body, which is a kind of integral sense organ before the division of the senses has occurred. It takes in the mother's emotions with its skin and becomes one with the mother; it feels her and is part of her, mother and foetus are one, communion becomes existence. "Communication appears to be on three levels [Verny 1982]: physiological, sympathetic and behavioural. Verny describes sympathetic communication as a form of extrasensory transmission between mother and foetus through her emotions, e.g. love and acceptance as well as her negative feelings ...

"Verny [1982] comments that the success of bonding depends upon maternal sensitivity regarding what she communicates to her unborn child, and what it communicates to her. He maintains that:

A strong intra-uterine bond is a child's ultimate protection against the outside world's dangers and uncertainties, and its effects are not limited to the uterine period ... All that comes afterwards hinges on what happens now, which is why it is so critical that mother and child remain attuned to each other." [5]

"When the moment of delivery arrives, the mother must be ready to create a new bond, and also to be available to enter that condition which Winnicott described as a state of total involvement in which mothers become able to 'step into the shoes of the baby'." [6]

"When there are periods of stress, such as a separation or mistimed interaction (misattunement), this can be repaired if followed by a synchronised (attuned) interaction." [7] "Changes in the infant's levels of arousal are related to changes in metabolic energy, which affects brain growth. Therefore, this regulation of affective states has an impact upon the organisation of the right hemisphere of the brain, particularly the frontal limbic regions, during a period of rapid growth." [8] "This part of the brain is dominant during the early postnatal period [Trevarthen 1996]. It is associated with the regulation of affect and the perception of the emotional states of others, and 'is believed to be responsible for the development of reciprocal relations in mother-infant regulatory systems'. It is the place where the early internal working models of the attachment relationship are stored." [9]

Teresa A. Cottrell writes:

"In my research I have accessed material which suggests that negative environmental factors can affect the relationship between mother and foetus *in utero*. I suggest that the negative environment is one where the mother is not sufficiently sensitively responsive and cannot provide the continuity of protection for the foetus from impingements. In other words, there is insufficient attunement between mother and foetus. This may be, for example, because the mother does not want a baby or because her own psychic state makes her unavailable emotionally. Verny [1982] refers to Fedor-Freybergh's report regarding Kristina, a healthy neonate who refused her mother's breast whilst eagerly accepting that of another mother. Investigation revealed that Kristina's mother had not wanted to be pregnant; she had wanted an abortion, but had the child because her husband wanted it. Verny comments that Kristina had been aware of the rejection; she had been shut out emotionally in the womb, and was protecting herself from her mother, and was refusing to bond with her." [10] ...

"Negative maternal emotions can represent another impingement, whether experienced physiologically through chemicals, or through the sound and rhythm of the mother's voice" ... [11] "Verny comments that the risk to bonding occurs when the mother withdraws into herself, becoming distracted by her own emotional pain, and is unable to reassure the foetus. He demonstrates that maternal anger, anxiety and fear will prompt furious kicking from the foetus, and if unresolved, can make bonding difficult." ...

"Weinstock [1997] shows that exposure to uncontrollable psychological stress during the prenatal period causes an insult to the hypothalamic-pituitary-adrenal axis, which results in behavioural changes in children, including attention deficit hyperactivity disorder, hyperanxiety and disturbed social behaviour. It may also increase the risk of developing endogenous depression" [12] ...

"An example of a misattunement is demonstrated by Murray's TV replay test, which showed that a two month old becomes distressed and avoidant if the mother's behaviour, however friendly and expressive, is inappropriate in timing and unreactive to what the baby is doing" [Murray, 1980; Murray and Trevarthen, 1985; Trevarthen, 1985a]. This is demonstrated further in the video-taped interaction of the 'still face' situation [Brazelton and Cramer, 1991], during which the mother presents her infant with a completely still face, not responding to it in any way. The results are that:

> "The consistent pattern of infant behaviour in the still-face situation is repeated attempts to elicit mother's response, followed by sombre expression, orientation away from mother, and finally withdrawal. After initial efforts and initial protest, they collapse into a self-protective state. First, they try to avoid the need they have to look at their mother. Then they try to 'turn off' their environment completely. Finally, they try their own techniques of self-comforting." [13]

"In Winnicott's terms, I suggest that this behaviour could be the infant's reaction to impingements, from which it is not being protected due to the loss of the 'holding' mother. It would represent a failure in the holding environment, leaving the infant exposed to 'unthinkable anxiety' (going to pieces, falling forever, having no relationship to the body, having no orientation), and resulting in a break in the infant's 'going-on-being'. If the infant has to react to an excess of impingements, it experiences a threat of annihilation, which produces a very primitive (existential) anxiety." [14]

"Bowlby associated insecure attachment with various forms of psychopathology including anxiety and depression as well as phobias, for example, agoraphobia and school phobia." [15]

If we ask what the basic needs of human beings are, we find them even before an individual is born into the world: the need for love, warmth, protection, for awareness of its feelings and the mother's responsiveness, her happiness with the yet unborn baby and empathy with it. At that stage the mother and the womb in which it lives are the whole world, and even after it is born the mother still represents the whole world to the baby. When it feels the mother's good feelings it responds with satisfaction and expansiveness, its body organs and its brain will develop to their full potential, but it will react with fear and anxiety if it feels her rejection, and its bodily organs will contract and inhibit physical and emotional self-expression and development.

To put it simply, the radiations of the mother's libido, its affirmative and negating aspects will envelop the foetus, which not only responds to them but also internalises and makes them its own. But while structure of the brain and of the body is genetically inherited, their function, particularly that of the brain, is influenced by the emotions and states of mind which influence the neurological and chemical processes of the nervous system and the body's physiological functions. But even while, as we have seen, a person's experiences in the uterus have a major impact upon his physical and mental characteristics, they must not be considered as final. After birth many changes in the mother-baby relationship can occur, and the child's capacity for compensation and sublimation can produce new variations in its behaviour and the way it copes with its life in the world outside.

The Newborn's Communion with the World Outside.

At birth the infant is expelled from the universe of the womb, to which it has become accustomed during its evolution from a fertilised cell to a human being, to confront an entirely unfamiliar and strange existence. However, nature provides the newborn with a crucial link with the new world outside by the hypersensitisation of the lips upon which its libidinous needs are focussed. The mother's breast in the first instance replaces the umbilical cord for the supply of nourishment and contact, and the infant's mouth and lips become the focus for its survival, even while the whole body communion with the mother's radiation continues to operate. The mouth and the lips feel the instinctive drive to make contact with the breast and the nipple, which sets in motion the sucking reflex which has been established prenatally. We can observe that many embryos suck their fingers, usually the thumb, during the last six weeks or so of the intra-uterinal existence, and some are even born with their thumb in their mouth.

The infant's lips, embracing and sucking at the mother's breast, are meant to stimulate libidinous response from the mother which, in turn, arouses in the child sensations of satisfaction and pleasure. The infant takes in the mother's libido from her breast, and recognises it as an internal, physical experience; it incorporates not only the milk from the mother but the libido that comes from her breast and from her whole being. Melanie Klein has frequently pointed to the fact that it is not only the nourishment, the milk, which is all-important. It is the child's sensation of her libido, her feelings of pleasure and joyfulness, or her state of anxiety and, indeed, the whole state of mind which the child incorporates and becomes aware of as an internal experience.

Indeed, the lips are quite extraordinarily sensitive; they are the focus of the child's libido, and we might say that it feels and knows with its lips, that its whole information and orientation system is centred upon them. Connected with the sensations of the lips and mouth is the sensation of taste. We have to adjust our grown-up concept of taste in order to understand the infant, for it not only tastes the physical sensations of the nipple and the milk but above all the quality of its mother's libido and her often unconscious attitudes towards the child. Her feelings of pleasure and joy will make her nipple and her milk taste sweet and pleasant, while anxious or rejective attitudes will produce in the child a sour or bitter or unpleasant taste. This taste experience will in turn produce expansive, joyful and trustful, or frightened, contractive and rejective reactions. Sour taste evokes tension and tightness in the lips, whereas a sweet taste will produce expansive reactions in the musculature, as in a smile, which we can recognise as an expression of pleasure.

These primary responses involve the whole incorporative system and spread from the lips to the mouth, to the jaws, the throat, the oesophagus, the solar plexus and the stomach. For, after all, these are the channels by which the life-providing processes take place, and it is particularly the stomach which receives the nourishment and its libido, and it will replicate the sensations of the lips as well as their physiological responses. Sour and repulsive sensations in the lips produce sour, repulsive and anxious sensations in the stomach. We can say that the lips, which for the infant are the first to establish contact with the world outside, evaluate with their sense of taste its life outside the womb and act as a signalling system to which all the incorporative activities respond. The way the world tastes indicates whether it loves the child, whether the child is accepted and loved, and whether it can love itself. Mother's good feeling makes the child feel good, expansive and accepted, and the stomach will enact those feelings. If the world – primarily represented by the mother – feels good and tastes good, then the baby itself feels good, and if the world feels bad, baby feels bad.

Let me reiterate the basic principle that if the mother withdraws her libido, then the baby's libido withdraws, and with it the organic function associated with the intake process pulls back, withdraws and tightens up. But these responses evoke fear and will manifest themselves in rage, choking, breathlessness, rigidities of the peripheral and back muscles, outbursts of aggression, tantrums, and what could later turn into epileptic fits.

Aggression and rage is a response of the organism to the withdrawal of libido that is experienced as a barrier to gratification, which the infant has to penetrate, in order to make contact with the feelings of life, which have disappeared or have remained hidden. Biting, screaming and kicking as well as an increase in blood pressure are mechanisms of aggression designed to release the organism from its tension and to counteract the withdrawal reflex. We can say that primary aggression in its many manifestations is a way of getting access to libidinous responses, a signalling system indicating the infant's needs, as well as a release from its blocks and tensions, and to gain access to the libido that has been denied. Unless these expressions of the infant's fears and aggressiveness gain the appropriate response from the parents in terms of reassurance and warmth, they are likely to become fixated and lay the foundations to the individual's future physiological structure and his reflexes and, eventually, for his psychological and also his social characteristics.

Freud maintained that the baby is not aware of the mother as a separate object, but only of its own urges and feelings. He was correct that it is not aware of the mother as a separate object, but greatly underestimated the baby's awareness of the mother's sensations and feelings and the way it incorporates them and identifies with them. In my investigations of the newborn's sensations under hypnosis I could observe the baby's extraordinary awareness of the mother's state of mind and her attitude towards it. The extraordinary sensitivity of the baby in the first instance in its lips, and the physiological awareness of the attitudes and feelings of its mother, the overwhelming power of the earliest experiences were revealed to their full extent: its terrors and its rages, the need to attack the world which does not want it, its urge to bite the non-giving nipple in order to get a response, and on the other hand, a sense of security, happiness, expansiveness in the embrace of a loving universe. We enter here the world of the id with its cauldron of impulses and emotions of which Freud has spoken, but which he regarded as a kind of given entity, without understanding its nature and its causes. As I said, the infant does not 'know' during the pre-ego stage what it experiences and what its body does, it just happens and the baby has no defence against it.

What is of interest to us here in particular is that the reflexes of the infant are imprinted in the nervous system and continue to operate unconsciously, involuntarily, as people grow up and what is more colour their perceptions of reality and patterns of behaviour, which have their roots in the involuntary reflexes of infancy. The baby does not know it is doing it – "*It* happens," said Groddeck, which he, and then Freud, called *das Es* (translated as 'the id' in Freud's case and as 'the It' in Groddeck's).

The Sense of Self: Narcissism and the Ego Functions.

With the emergence of a sense of self, the child begins to feel in terms of '*I* want', '*I* want to be fed, receive love and attention from mother' and – with the growing awareness of the father's existence – 'from him' and from other members of the family and from the world. With a sense of self, the child will no longer think in terms of '*it* feels cold' or hungry or rejected but '*I* feel cold' or hungry or frightened or on the other hand, '*I* feel good', and '*I* feel that mother is happy with me'. The child needs to reach out and embrace the mother and feel her body and those of other members of the family and re-establish body contact. It is, however, crucial for its further psychological development that if it feels deprived of body contact, it will embrace itself, so to speak, by tightening up its periphery, it will hold on to itself to acquire a sense of security and even to feel that it exists. If the expansive urge of the libido encounters resentment or rejection, the child learns to hide its libido and keeps it for itself. Such people frequently become tight, stubborn and mean in expressing their feelings; pedantic and carefully calculating about what they can show of themselves, they do not trust themselves to open up to others or to touch, and have to protect or repress their libidinous needs, finding it difficult to show them. Keeping oneself to oneself, not intruding upon others, keeping one's privacy and at best respecting the privacy of others can become a cultural value, but it frequently leads to an impairment of empathy and lack of awareness of the feelings and needs of others. There are many variations in which such responses can develop in the life of a person or indeed of a culture.

If the armoured, tight periphery becomes too powerful it becomes a barrier to self-expression. Such individuals feel imprisoned by their own armour and will want to attack it, and become aggressive in order to break down this wall surrounding them, a wall of indifference towards their own emotional needs. Children who do not receive sufficient attention and body contact will eventually feel neglected by the world, will be unable to reach out and embrace, will attack the wall of indifference, and seek contact by means of aggression and violence. If they attack they exist, they are being taken notice of, they are important.

It is interesting to note that the egocentric character of which I have spoken which lacks awareness of other people's needs and upholds the virtues of privacy and of looking after one's self, becomes the role model of capitalist democracy imbued with a culture of individualism and free enterprise. But all too often individualism is centred upon a strong libidinous cathexis on the self – selfishness – with a diminishing awareness of the narcissistic needs of others who become objects to be used for the promotion of self-interest. Such individuals will form communities of self-important people, and 'the others', who are not successful in the competition for personal power and recognition, will either have to identify with the glamorous narcissists and submit to them, or rebel against them. 'I rebel, therefore I am', said Camus. The self-centred people will identify with others of their type in clubs, professions and select groups and organisations and keep ordinary people out, but will find ways of using them in politics, in wars, in business and financial operations as human fodder to satisfy their narcissistic ambitions.

But I am racing ahead to the world of grown-ups, and I shall return to it later. It is almost irresistible to observe the baby in the grown-up, for there is a baby in all of us which influences our attitudes, our values and our behaviour, even while we are careful not to be conscious of it.

With the development of the ego functions begins a process of unifying the multitude of impulses into a coherent sense of self and, as the capacity to synthesise grows stronger, the strength of the co-ordinating capacity of the ego increases. The sense of I is no longer restricted to an awareness of what I want at this moment and the response I receive, as the awareness of time, past and future, spatial relationships, consequences of actions, cause and effect, experiment and play, and the boundaries of what one can do and what one cannot do, emerge. These boundaries can be a source of security – an embrace of the possible, or a source of irritation, frustration or anger, depending on how the sense of self was encouraged and supported.

Besides the fundamental signalling system of taste transmitted by the lips, all the other senses operate in the process of our physiological responses. Taste interacts with a sense of vision, smell, hearing and touch. In other words, we take into ourselves the world around us (not merely receive passively, but actively reach out and incorporate) with all our senses. The visual sense is activated from the second or third day, but the baby does not see as we can see; as its cortical system is not yet connected with the visual sense, it is not able to recognise the specific configuration and meaning of objects. However, while the infant does not perceive the objects around it, it will receive sensations which emanate from them. It will react strongly to pleasant or unpleasant colours or shapes, and experience them in its body. Light colours, if they are not too glaring, will produce expansive, pleasurable feelings, as will harmonious, soft shapes, while sudden, sharp movements, represented by sharp, edgy shapes, will produce anxiety and often panic. As grown-ups we still look for warm, harmonious patterns which we find pleasurable and reassuring in landscape and architecture, while paintings quite clearly symbolise certain emotional meanings by their colours and configurations. Just think of the contrast between a Raphael and a Francis Bacon, quite apart from the actual content of the picture. We seek an environment, landscape or urban architecture which is relaxing, expansive, accepting and assuring, and want to escape from the disharmonies and sharp, harassing and grey, colourless world that surrounds us in many areas and is reproduced in modern art.

The magic of touch: again the contrast between the aggressive or mean or tight and loveless touch, as against the warm and loving contact with another living being. We speak of green fingers, and it seems that even vegetables and flowers respond to a loving hand that handles them, and of course all animals seek body contact and a caressing touch, and animal lovers are well aware of this. As for the sense of sound, it is interesting to note that when I regressed some patients to the embryonic state after the seventh month, the most pronounced sensations they reported were the sounds of the mother's heartbeat and the symphonic cacophony of her digestive tract and breathing. What was even more startling was the embryo's acute response to the mother's state of anxiety, manifested in the irregularity of her breathing and her heartbeat.

The impact of sound upon our emotions is of course well known, and music as well as singing represent to us the whole range of emotions which we can experience. Farmers speak to their animals, and it seems to be true that cows yield more milk if they are made to feel good with pleasant music or singing. It is also true that there is music in all of us, even though the form of music which we harbour in our souls and which we seek out varies considerably. One speaks of these things as God-given or, in more fashionable terms, as being genetically inherited. However, even as God claims to have given us a measure of free will, and cannot be held responsible for every nastiness or stupidity perpetrated by his human creations, so genetic programming allows for a wide range of variability in the human personality. The more one investigates the psychological factor, the more one has to recognise its impact upon the development of a person's character.

While I have mentioned the positive response to warm and harmonious visual as well as sound and touch sensations, it is nevertheless true to say that many people are drawn towards aggressive, jagged, dark images and seem to enjoy them in architecture as well as in paintings. Who can doubt that much of what goes for music in our time is aggressive and brutal, jagged and disharmonious, and increasingly accompanied by a kind of dancing which is jerky, aggressive, sudden in its movement and seems to defy all notion of harmony, softness and beauty. Indeed, we find that much of musical entertainment is associated with violent bodily movement ('power dancing' and 'spastic dancing'), which reminds one of infantilistic expressions of anger, defiance and outrage. Acting out tantrums and spasms seems to be a favourite musical art form which expresses popular feelings in a desublimated expression, of which I have spoken as characteristic of small children.

Let me reiterate that on the deepest, infantile and unconscious level, the individual derives his identity from the primary object whose libido he incorporates and feels inside himself. We have seen that pleasurable sucking, the sensations of the libido of the breast and the milk will provide a sense of gratification in the child which feels the good object inside itself and will feel good. The sensation of the bad libido emanating from the mother will arouse aggressive forms of incorporation with tooth and claw. Aggression towards the object becomes, through the process of internalisation, aggression against the self.

While the satisfying experience of the release of aggression towards an object is a basis of sadism, aggression towards the internalised object turns sadism into masochism. This not only produces a wide range of paranoias, anxieties and forms of self-hatred as well as inadequacy feelings, but also many physiological disturbances and tensions, which one could call forms of auto-aggression. One does to the internal object – the self – what one wants to do to the external object, which one has introjected. Individuals like this will experience painful cramps in the solar plexus and stomach whenever they are angry, whenever they encounter situations they 'cannot stomach', cannot accept, and will attack the internal bad object. The early responses of the infant tend to become structured into reflexes, and largely determine a person's subsequent physical as well as psychological characteristics.

Development and Transformations of the Libido.

A person's character development is not merely a matter of the contingencies and accidents of his environmental conditions. There is a certain innate direction in every person's psycho-biological evolution, which Freud called the development and transformations of the libido. He found that the libido undergoes a number of transformations in the course of a person's development from infancy to adulthood, and that, furthermore, these transformations occur with considerable regularity in all individuals. The regularity of libidinous transformations emboldened Freud to formulate a law of sexual development which has since found ample confirmation in the psychoanalysis of children and adults. However, he also discovered that a person's development can be arrested at a certain stage of his evolution, and that his development may be blocked and produce a wide range of neurotic conflicts.

It is one of the cornerstones of psychoanalytic theory that the sexual drive, or libido, is not confined to genital sexuality, that children are not sexless, as had been assumed, but that there exists in the child a wide spectrum of sexual drives and that at certain periods of his development certain drives become dominant, i.e. attain primacy over others. While the sexual drive exists from the very beginning of a person's life, it is connected to a wide range of vital functions and has to pass through a complicated process before it attains the characteristics of what we call the normal genital sexuality of adults. Sexuality thus is not an instinct that manifests itself in a particular form only but is more like an energy that undergoes many transformations in an individual's life.

In my book *The Unknown Self* I deal with the development of the libido in the individual, its disturbances and conflicts, and it forms the background to my therapeutic method:

"In the development of individuals, in the unfolding of their organic and psychic potential, the libido attaches itself to a succession of activities, and at various stages gives them primacy over the others. By means of the libidinous urges the individual is compelled to follow the needs of the organism. It is as if nature had provided a pleasure-seeking energy that attaches itself to the important self-preserving and species-preserving activities, and motivates these activities by an almost irresistible drive, which, if fulfilled, rewards the organism with a sense of pleasure, while frustration or denial arouses sensations of anxiety, aggressiveness and tension.

While the species-preserving functions of the individual in the form of genital sexuality are given high emphasis by nature, it is necessary for the individual, as a link in the chain of the life of a species, to preserve itself and to develop its potentials, and for that purpose the self-preserving functions and those directed to the growth and the development of the individual organism are cathexed with sufficient quanta of libido to ensure that they are carried out. In the development of the individual, in the process of its evolution and growth, libidinous energy is channelled to a succession of vitally necessary functions. We can define the development of the pregenital libido as serving the purpose of:

1) directing the child towards oral activities for the incorporation of food and communion with mother;

2) establishing the child's awareness of itself as a separate and distinct individual by making the self an object of libidinous gratification. We call this primacy narcissism, and it is the foundation for the development of the ego and a sense of self;

3) establishing the process of self-projection, which is motivated by the anal libido, assuring the child of its sense of identity in the world and its capacity of producing and manipulating objects."

We might say that the early primacies of the libido serve the preservation and development of the individual, and at the conclusion of the development devoted to individual self-preservation there occurs a concentration of libido upon the genitals. Of course the pregenital or infantile primacies of the libido do not cease to operate with the advent of sexual maturity, nor is the genital libido absent in infancy. At certain stages of his development the individual is dominated by a libidinous primacy, but the so-called normal person is able to develop further, and in some measure enter the next stage on the scale of his personal evolution. In the neurotic personality the degree of fixation is more pronounced and will continue to dominate him. He remains stuck, so to speak, in a halfway house on the road of his psychic development and will face the world with the expectations and desires of his infantile primacies, and the development of his ego will be impaired. The so-called normal person's character will also be influenced by certain primacies, but he will be able to sublimate and accommodate them to the needs of reality, a process which is the chief task of the ego. As can be seen, I am employing here an evolutionary model in the aetiology of neurosis as well as of character. Neither character nor neurotic symptoms should be taken as fixed phenomena, either genetically determined or divinely ordained and classified as static entities. In keeping with the classic psychoanalytic model, I am concerned with their history.

While I have drawn attention to the infant's primary physiological responses in the process of internalisation, it is not long before the mind is activated and physiological processes are expressed in psychological terms. The physiological processes continue to operate but they are picked up by the mind and transformed into psychological activity. And by psychological, we mean thoughts, images, fantasies, apprehension, fear, horror, pleasure, desire, sense of isolation, or confidence and security.

As the sensorium is gradually connected with the cortical and prefrontal functions, sensations become perceptions, reflexes are largely transformed into volition, and the mind creates a new territory of experience, the sense of self and with it the ego functions begin to develop.

The Receiving and the Giving Mode.

However, there is another way of gaining identity and narcissistic gratification, namely by what one produces. We must bear in mind that the task of identity acquisition is of particular importance in human beings as their responses and orientations in relationship to their environment are not fully determined by instinctual programming. During the oral primacy of the libido, identification takes place through the introjection of the mother's libido and nourishment, and the child is what it receives and incorporates. In the narcissistic phase the libido is directed to its own body periphery; it acquires a self-image, a sense of self by libidinous body contact, and the attention of people to feed its self-love. During the anal primacy which follows, it identifies with what it produces, i.e. it projects itself outside, and then identifies with the object it has produced. The object which comes out of it will arouse its curiosity and fascination. We may call the early development of the libido – from the union of the embryo with its mother to the oral and the narcissistic stages of its development – the receiving mode. The child depends for its survival upon what it receives and the ego's co-ordination into a coherent sense of self. The early stages of the libido serve the preservation of the individual and the acquisition of its sense of identity.

The acquisition of identity by what one produces, which I call the giving mode, plays an important part in the life of individuals and of societies.

In order to understand the psychological problems which the anal libido encounters, we must remember the close interaction between the processes of internalisation and projection. If the breast as well as the mother's periphery gave out – projected – satisfying libido sensations, they will be introjected by the child, they become part of the child's self and engender a good self-feeling. In this case, the anal projections represent the good self coming out into the world, and the child will want to present it to the mother, and later to the world, as a gift-offering. This we may call the pleasurable, self-affirmative form of self-projection. Love is returned for love, pleasure for pleasure, self-projection and production will be experienced as a pleasurable, creative act to be shared with others. The bad libido, on the other hand, and the rejective attitudes experienced, will emerge in its form of self-projection. It may want to deprive the mother and the world by withholding its product and adopt a variety of anal-retentive mechanisms. It will become stubborn, obstinate and even spiteful. This trait leads to hoarding, compulsive saving, and the unconscious mind of such a person will say: 'I haven't received anything really warm and loving and good, so I will not give out anything, I will not give till I receive. I will hide what is in me, I will not let anyone know what I have, what I think or what I feel. I cannot show my innermost self without embarrassment and fear of criticism and rejection.'

These conflicts can also lead to anal-aggressiveness, in the same way as oral tensions frequently lead to oral-aggressive-cannibalistic drives. The child will want to throw its faeces at the world, to soil it as 'a load of shit' and make it suffer the agonies of being despised as it has been made to feel. Such people will become 'muck-rakers' and develop a sharp eye for people's weaknesses, a talent to humiliate and make them feel dirty, inadequate or nasty. If as a child it has been made to experience parental disgust with and rejection of the product it has produced and made to feel that it is itself disgusting and dirty, it anticipates that whatever it produces, or any ambitions it may have, would be rejected with a kind of contempt. It will be frightened of showing the world whatever it may want to do.

Anal defiance and anal-aggressive drives play a large role not only in certain individuals but also in subcultures devoted to rebellious attitudes. People who as members of a social class or ethnic group have experienced narcissistic injury, a sense of deprivation and insult to their dignity, will show opposition to the social establishment by insulting the accepted norms of good manners. They will pollute – degrade – the hostile environment by either actually throwing dirt at it (as we can see in many examples of contemporary art), or will wear torn or shabby clothes, or behave and talk in a dirty, obscene, defiant manner. We can indeed speak of the proliferation of an anal-aggressive subculture in times of social conflict.

But apart from such extreme manifestations of the anal libido, the child will learn to discriminate between acceptable and not acceptable, desirable and undesirable objects, and there is the desire to possess the former, to collect, to count and to exchange them, to enhance the value of one's possessions. The child is much preoccupied with defining, separating and categorising objects.

The rule games – of which there are an almost infinite variety among children and among grown-ups, as for instance the playing of cards, chess and dominoes as well as sporting competitions, and more recently, playing the stock exchange and financial manipulations – originate out of an emotional need to impose order on a confusing environment. It also enables people to distinguish between what is analogous and what is not, what can be connected with what, and what is separate, and the concept of unification and specification leads to logical operations. The foundation of logic lies in the distinction between *A* and *non-A*, and the criteria by which we can judge *A* to be separate from *non-A*. Such distinctions relate not only to objects but also to concepts and to logical categories by which we judge objects as well as actions and ideas of objects and actions. They become rules for cognitive discrimination and eventually develop into criteria for what is true or false, good or bad, clean or dirty.

As soon as a culture establishes a consensus of the meaning of numbers and the worth of material objects, men can collect and evaluate objects; they may buy and sell, invest and make profit. This ability is not an invention of capitalism, but capitalism is an expression and further development of this capability and provides enhanced motivation for its exercise, giving it domination over all other considerations. In particular, it transforms the act of production, its products as well as the people who have produced them.

The producer who soils himself in his labours is not recognised in the product he has made, and the products themselves are no longer connected with the producer who has made them. The capitalists take the workers' product away from them and make it their own possession, thereby making it clean and desirable. They do not have to do the dirty work, they do not soil themselves by contact with dirty matter, they are the clean ones, the élite as distinguished from the earthbound, soiled, labouring peasant and working class. "The hierarchic system", as Nietzsche has observed, "centres around the clean and unclean, the pure man and the dirty man"; it reflects the conflicts of the anal libido, which finds expression in societies. In the hierarchical society the capitalists, like the old feudal rulers, not only take the things the workers have produced away from them and make themselves rich and esteemed, but also deny the workers the opportunity to identify with what they have produced. They encourage the 'common people' to identify with the élite and the rich and at the same time to project their own sense of dirtiness upon the 'others', the foreigners, the outsiders, to despise them and fight wars against them, like the Nazis, for instance, who declared that the dirty Jews threaten the purity of the German soul.

Obsession and Ritual.

There is yet another way which the child as well as the grown-up adopts in order to cope with anxieties aroused by the anal libido, namely obsessive undoing. Instead of splitting the ego from the unacceptable anal desires and sensations and projecting them upon the others, it will attempt to negate them by means of obsessive acts and ceremonials. For instance, the urge to handle and play with dirty things has to be counteracted by obsessive cleaning and washing of the hands or any part of the body that may have had contact with dirty things. Such negation takes the form of active rituals in order to overcome an otherwise unbearable anxiety. The child caught in overpowering anal taboos must attempt to cope with its anxieties by performing obsessive acts of denial and fending off its unclean urges. Adult society employs professionals to carry out the public ceremonials designed to propitiate and counteract the collective anxieties. The priests, rabbis or mullahs or, in secular societies, the rulers and bureaucrats uphold and impose institutionalised obsessions, and enforce its rituals.

The hierarchic system, as we have remarked, centres around the clean and the dirty, the superior and the lowly, the aristocrat and the plebeian. All rulers or ruling classes claim for themselves the charisma of purity and cleanliness with their perfumes and shiny clothes and sparkling jewellery, and they take care that the priests and bureaucrats perpetuate their image of purity in the minds of the population. The public rituals of cleansing and immersion in holy waters continue in a large variety of symbolic forms in our own time in the 'ideological theocracies', as for instance during the communist dictatorship of Soviet Russia, when every citizen had to read Karl Marx and was not considered cleansed from the obscenities of bourgeois or Christian prejudices unless he immersed himself in the holy texts of Marxist-Leninism. The ritual incantation of these texts in the educational system was no different from the priest's or the mullah's incantations, which the congregation has to repeat after him. We all have to mouth various magic sentences or slogans and have to learn them by heart, in order to be considered full members of our culture and accepted by the priests and king, the ruler or the political ideology of our party.

However, there is a fundamental difference between obsessive acts and the rational pursuit of cleanliness, just as there is a difference between obsessive mouthing of slogans and the rational exercise of the intellect. The former are circular and self-enclosed, while the latter are open-ended and unfolding. Indeed, the former prevent the exercise of rational thought-processes, and even the pursuit of cleanliness is inhibited by obsessive ritualisation, as can be seen in the dirty conditions of holy rivers. It is not cleanliness, wisdom or justice which obsessive ceremonials promote – cleanliness rituals have no more to do with the pursuit of cleanliness than the incantations of slogans have to do with the pursuit of the truth.

However, while projection, splitting and obsessiveness emerge with the anal primacy, they are not confined to it but are subsequently related to other areas. Once established as a mode of operation in the psychic apparatus, they appear in other libidinous primacies, and play a very important role in sexuality, as we can see in authoritarian, repressive societies where the indulgence in sexual pleasures is condemned as dirty.

We have seen that in the development of individuals, in the process of their evolution and growth, in the unfolding of their organic and psychic potential, the libido attaches itself to a succession of activities and at various stages gives them primacy over the others. By means of the libidinous urges the individual is compelled to follow the needs of the organism. It is as if nature had provided the pleasure-seeking energy that attaches itself to the important self-preserving and species-preserving activities. If fulfilled it rewards the organism with a sensation of pleasure, while frustration or denial arouses anxiety, anger, aggressiveness and sadism or obsessions.

Libidinous energy is channelled into vital functions, and we might say that the early transformations of the libido serve the preservation and development of the individual and gradually enable it to become a producer.

The Primacy of the Genital Libido.

During the next stage of its evolution the libido, or a very large part of it, is centred upon the genitals. The individual begins to transcend his self-preserving functions to ensure the life of the species, and by giving himself up to orgasm, he enters a moment of eternity. It is the ultimate form of the giving mode, not only in order to produce and affirm man's essential self in society and satisfy his narcissistic needs, but to create the future and ensure the life of humanity, of life itself. It is the affirmation of love, of Eros, the life-affirming libido; it participates in life beyond the confines of individuality, and by merging with the other person he transcends himself so to speak and partakes in the universal life of his species. This is not merely a poetic notion (although it is the perennial theme of poetry), but the description of an experience which characterises the life functions and the person's achievement of maturity. In his orgastic experience he not only experiences a moment of eternity but he creates eternity, both on the biological and psychological level. And the woman becomes the agent of eternity and the symbol of everlasting life, the being who ensures that life continues by drawing the male out of his confines.

The pre-genital erotic drives do not disappear but they lose their primacy, that is, their energies are subordinated to the genital impulse; they frequently stimulate and enhance them but gain their fulfilment through genital excitement and orgasm. That the infantile stages of the libido do not disappear during genital primacy is shown by the fact that in adult love-making erotic activities such as sucking, kissing, looking, smelling, touching and exploring, as well as the narcissistic need to be loved for oneself and being a producer and provider of the material necessities of life, play an important part. Every fulfilling sex act of a mature individual is, as it were, a recapitulation of the development of his libido.

However, while with the onset of puberty large amounts of the libido are directed to the genitals, in human beings the process of maturation is delayed. As cultures accumulate an ever greater store of knowledge and of skills, children have to be taught

40

and trained to master them, and can only be considered mature and able to take their place as full members of their society after they have received a measure of proficiency in the skills of their culture and become capable of handing them on to their offspring. Even at the age of thirteen, when the human being is sexually, i.e. reproductively, mature, he is still a child and continues to need the protection and love of his father and mother and guidance of his teachers. While the libido sends a massive flow of energy to the genitals, making its urges well-nigh irresistible, the boy or girl will not consider sexuality as being directed towards procreation but as an end in itself.

I should mention here that as an organ of erotogenic activity the genitals are active from birth onwards, and genital masturbation can be observed in infants. Indeed, we can speak of a first puberty at the age of five or six when large amounts of the libido are directed to the genitals, but the process of maturation is delayed in human beings until twelve or thirteen, when reproduction ability is actually established. In advanced societies like ours, the person cannot be considered mature or even grown up until he has acquired the skills and traditions of his culture. One must always remember that the development of the individual does not take place in a mechanical manner, i.e. one stage following another stage, but in a biological form, that is, all libidinous drives are present at the same time but one acquires primacy over the others during certain stages of his evolution.

However, the progression to higher stages of development rarely proceeds smoothly. Fixation upon early libidinous primacies can cause them to persist alongside newer primacies; if the libido encounters unresolved difficulties or fixations upon a certain stage it tends to regress to the earlier stages. Freud used the analogy of an advancing army in enemy territory leaving occupation troops at all important points: "The stronger the occupation troops left behind, the weaker is the army that marches on. If the latter meets a too powerful enemy force, it may retreat to those points where it had previously left the strongest occupation troops. The stronger a fixation, the more easily will a regression take place." (Sigmund Freud: *Introductory Lectures on Psychoanalysis*, Lecture 22).

The disturbances in the transition from one primacy to another occur in all individuals as newly emerging primacies are influenced by the older established patterns; the genital libido will always be influenced by the characteristics which pre-genital primacies have adopted. This is not merely a question of neuroticism or psychotic disturbances, it is a process which operates in the development of every person's character formation and will be reflected in the collective character of a society. Thus societies can regress to early infantile primacies and their culture be invaded by the fears and rages of childhood.

The Latency Period.

One can say that the latency period is a drawn-out period of gratification delay and enables the undischarged sexual urges to be sublimated into learning, skill acquisition and all kinds of disciplined activities. The great majority of communal activities, from work to sports, from study to the playing of games, are based upon rules which have to be accepted, for otherwise these activities would be meaningless. It is within the framework of rules that individual initiative can be exercised. Discipline, therefore, means that the individual is prepared to control the direct expression of instinctual drives and to sublimate them in order to satisfy the norms and rules of the parental superego and its social representatives such as trainers and teachers.

Beside the evocation of the anal libido for the purpose of learning to handle and make things in preparation for productive work, we find many other forms of the pregenital libido in the service of maturation. The process of learning and study reactivates the child's curiosity about life and the mysteries of birth and sex.

The urge to know things, how things relate to each other, what causes things to be the way they are, and to ask why and how things happen is basically motivated by sexual curiosity, now directed by discipline and planned enquiry. The urge to penetrate behind the surface of things and to find the deeper reality which underlies them represents also the reactivation of the oral-aggressive drives determined to penetrate through the barriers which surround the maternal libido. The drive to know, therefore, also means to penetrate the secrets of nature and to remove her veil.

We devour books, we take in knowledge and make it our own, we do not only want to penetrate the hidden secrets which make things happen the way they do, we also want to incorporate the thoughts of our father and to devour his knowledge. We not only want to open the veils which hide the secrets of mother nature but also make God, the Father, open one fold of his mantle after another to reveal to us the secrets of his power and let us share some of his knowledge.

And so we begin to ask all kinds of questions about God, of heaven and hell, where the world is going, where it comes from; we are ready to enact the rituals and ceremonials which our culture has adopted and affirm our relationship with the universal power beyond the confines of reality. The image of the universal father arouses immense fascination, for we realise that he is a greater father than our own and governs the big world which we are just beginning to discover. We begin to be acquainted with scientific discoveries about the nature of the world and are fascinated by the laws which govern the universe.

However, in the reactivation of the pregenital libido during the latency period, its characteristics and its conflicts will also re-emerge and will influence the progress of learning. For instance, if the anal retentive syndromes were pronounced during infancy the young person will usually develop a talent for craftsmanship but may find it difficult to finish a product or endlessly delay its completion in case he is made to part with it; or if fixations upon anal gratifications and the desire to handle faeces has not been sublimated and transferred to substitute material, then the fear of being unclean and dirty will create anxiety, and guilt feelings will inhibit the child's ability to manipulate objects and the acquisition of skills will be impaired. The child will become extremely awkward, drop objects or handle them wrongly as if afraid to touch them, and generally develop all kinds of work impediments. Anal retentive fixations can also inhibit spontaneity and create an over-dependency on authoritative rules and being told what to do. Persons dominated by such characteristics will demand permission from the superego for any kind of action, will rely on exact instructions and need the reassurance of being given orders. (If such traits tend to characterise a culture, then it will be ready to submit to authoritarian rules).

Pronounced oral-aggressive dispositions in childhood can, on the other hand, produce an intensified urge for study and acquisition of knowledge. Freud has spoken of the disposition to analyse things as an expression of the oral-aggressive urge to attack objects and take them to pieces. The satisfaction which this activity provides is re-enacted in the satisfaction of analysing whole chunks of knowledge into its component parts; it also gives the satisfaction of crushing dogmas or established prejudices, or, by taking things to pieces to see what is inside them, the analytic mind gets immense satisfaction in observing the parts of the whole and the way they interact.

However, the exercise of discipline and acceptance of rules (such as the commandments of logic and empirical evidence), is a precondition for all types of learning. The latency period can therefore be regarded as the civilising period *par excellence*. It enables the young adolescent to submit to the demands of the superego and its social representatives and the requirements of the maturation process in preparation for civilised adulthood. In his *Essay on Criticism*, Alexander Pope wrote: "True ease in writing comes from art, not chance, as those move easiest who have learned to dance." When an admirer of the twelve-year-old Mozart expressed amazement about the natural ease of his piano playing, young Mozart called him a fool, and angrily retorted that it took him many years of hard practise to obtain his mastery.

However, there occur situations when the power of the superego, both in its individual and in its social representation, is significantly weakened, ceases to be convincing and evokes widespread defiance. Then regression to earlier, infantile primacies will be enhanced and the rules by which they become sublimated into learning and skill acquisition are undermined. The individual's ability to concentrate will be profoundly impaired, he will be unable to accept discipline, and will turn against study, school and the authorities which make demands upon him. A restless search for immediate gratification and dissociative behaviour will dominate his personality. He will defy the rules and his teachers, he will be unable to study, he will be bored, aggressive or withdrawn. Such traits can emerge most powerfully during adolescence in the form of hooliganism or delinquency and other patterns of defiance, as in the epidemic of attention deficit, and present a major problem in a culture which has lost the confidence and power to convince young people and guide them towards standards of civilised modes of behaviour. We find many aspects of this in our contemporary societies where we can speak of the breakthrough of the repressed and regression to many aspects of infantilism.

God has made Adam and Eve leave paradise and go out into the world, to grow up and acquire the skills and the wisdom to recreate paradise on earth by their own effort, to affirm and to love life on this God-given planet.

We can say that while the Garden of Eden represents the childhood of humanity where the omnipotent Father and Mother Earth amply provide for its needs, the expulsion from Eden represents the latency period which enables humans to grow up, in order that they can cultivate the earth and make it blossom and unite mankind in the enjoyment of their humanity. Then God's purpose – the life-force Eros – will be realised, and with the unfolding of men's true destiny, real history – the Messianic age – will emerge.

CHAPTER 3

The Lost Vision of the Future

But it seems that we are not prepared to make the effort to achieve maturity and a measure of wisdom, as this would disturb our habits and many of our social institutions and would demand some sacrifices. In any case it would need a vision of the future. Very few now believe in the promise of heavenly rewards for the miseries we have to endure on this earth, while the messianic message of socialism with the inevitable movement of history towards the classless society as proclaimed by Marx no longer carries conviction. The hopes of the liberal philosophers of the nineteenth century that the freedom of private enterprise as enshrined in capitalist economy would produce a world of plenty in which all can eventually share have failed to fulfil their promises. The ancient theology as well as the modern ideologies can be seen to have failed in the experiments of history and have left us puzzled, disappointed and cynical. We feel that there is no point in waiting for the future, we want paradise now. And paradise means to receive everything we need or desire now, during our own life. And thus we are stuck in the receiving mode of childhood.

But there is a paradox here. While we have lost the vision of mankind's self-transcendence to realise its ultimate destiny in the future, we find ourselves in a world where our productive powers, a thousand times enhanced by science and technology, have also failed to fulfil our expectations. There seems no limit to our ability to control and shape the natural environment and transform matter into artefacts and commodities, to satisfy our ever-growing demands. Everything is possible and every whim and desire can be satisfied. With the explosion of productive capacity there is an equal expectation explosion, as what used to be merely a dream only a hundred years ago is now reality and within reach of everybody. There is a plenitude of satisfactions to be had: instant warmth and light by pressing a button, instant hot and cold water, bathrooms for every family, cheap, pre-cooked meals available at any time, medicines for every possible ailment assuring health and a long life, instant communication and information on every conceivable topic by computer technology, television, newspapers, journals and mass-produced books are available to everybody. The whole planet is now a playground open to the young to spend their holidays, to have fun and get to know the world, or to the elderly to alleviate their boredom; or, if one cannot be bothered spending half a day travelling to Paris for a shopping trip, one can go with the Internet and have full access to the best shops and be shown the best restaurants at the press of a button, and order whatever you wish via e-mail. And still we are discontented, frustrated and confused.

Life without the Latency Period.

Whereas in the old days – and not so long ago – novelists and psychoanalysts devoted their creative imagination and serious researches to the suffering of young people caused by the indomitable taboos imposed by civilisation upon their sexual urges, now, almost suddenly, all restraints are removed; boys as well as girls, men and women, are encouraged to proclaim their sexual urges in public via a large assortment of journals and newspapers and television programmes. 'One orgasm is not enough', proclaims the headline in an article about our search for sexual gratification, where women complain about the laziness and sexual incompetence of their lover, and are taught to handle his penis to make it more responsive and satisfying for their needs. And if this still does not achieve the desired result, we can have lessons in manual stimulation for multiple orgasms, with particular reference to the clitoris and the G-spot. Sexual liberation indeed! There is no time to be wasted in getting to know the person behind the penis, and there is no word about love. Instant gratification for all our needs at whatever age, whether those of puberty or of maturity which in the past were closely guarded secrets, is the new virtue.

With the abolition of the latency period and the rule of delayed gratification, which is the foundation for cultural aspirations, we find impulse-dominated behaviour. The most advanced areas of the brain – the frontal lobes which serve the need for foresight and anticipation of the results of our behaviour, the capacity which enabled our ancestors to make tools and put us in a commanding position over all animals to choose and discriminate between a multitude of drives, to succeed in the battle for survival in an often adverse and dangerous environment, making us the supreme creation of nature – are being sidelined and ignored in the rush for immediate gratification. If the frontal lobes of the brain are not activated or, as neurologists put it, fired into action, our intellectual and moral considerations will atrophy, with catastrophic consequences both to individuals and civilisation.

Immediate gratification does not enhance our well-being; our sense of achievement through the exercise of our human potential is lost and our self-respect with it. There is no sense of purpose or meaning in the world but a depressive feeling of having lost something fundamental in our existence, and we do not know what it is we have lost. We do not know why, but we feel the sense of futility in our obsessive rush to find satisfaction in an apparently indifferent world. We do not identify with what we make, our labours are only incidental to the overriding aim of making money as we sell our labours to the highest available bidder in a frantic race to acquire wealth and the prestige that goes with it.

In the 'old days' when there was little opportunity for young people to get rich quick, a working man or intellectual would be proud of what he does and his contribution to the needs of the community. Now he can only be proud of what he is worth in terms of the amount of money he receives. Young people are only too ready to sell whatever skills or knowledge they have, and do not ask for what purposes a business, a government or an international corporation will use their talents and abilities. The young out of school or university are keen to sell their talent for whatever purpose their paymasters have in mind, even if it means making fools of themselves to amuse the public, wearing outrageous and ridiculous clothes and exhibiting their sexual attraction, or acting as macho crackheads or lunatic comedians. The role models of our decadent society are puppets without personality, their appearance prefabricated to appeal and arouse the attention of what is assumed to be the public taste. The young thus become the cannon fodder for the wheeler dealers, as long as they are paid well and put into the limelight in the frantic rush to gain recognition in an otherwise anonymous existence.

The narcissistic hunger for recognition and fame, however, often borders on mania, which is a compensation for narcissistic deprivation and is frequently accompanied by depression in the preconscious awareness of the futility of their lives. Appearance is all, and the sense of self disappears behind the public act they adopt. It is no wonder that many of them become drug addicts and self-destructive in order to quell their feeling of disillusionment. And this not only applies to young people who are in the limelight, but also to mature people who are successful, wealthy and renowned.

The morning after I wrote this passage I felt that I was exaggerating: it may indeed apply to young people trying to find a career for themselves 'to get the best out of life', but it cannot apply to responsible business people, chairmen of large enterprises or professionals whose work must surely be devoted to the advancement of their companies or their clients. But then, the same morning, I read that Sir Roger Hurn did not consider being chairman of Marconi sufficiently rewarding for his talents: "He came to the job with a reputation as a sound manager who could be trusted to oversee the modernisation of the GEC. But [he] had other concerns. Being chairman of a company ... is not a full-time job: heavens, it only pays £295,000, plus almost as much again in pension contributions. So Sir Roger has to fill in his week ... with being chairman of Prudential, a director of ICI and joint deputy chairman of Glaxo SmithKline. And who could refuse an invitation to join the board of the élite stockbroking firm of Cazenove? Sir Roger certainly could not." [1]

This is a story a thousand times repeated in modern industry and commerce, and it is perhaps no wonder that it is reflected in the abysmal incompetence that pervades leading enterprises, which seem unable to focus their minds and their energies on the work they are expected to perform. The collapse of Marconi is just one example. "The other directors [of this company] have sat quietly through many of Britain's worst examples of corporate mismanagement, on boards from British Airways to British Telecom" ... (Patience Wheatcroft: *The Times* 17 July 2001).

This spectacle of the ruthless, obsessive drive for power and wealth is not confined to Britain. An even more massive manifestation of corruption among its directors and financial manipulators has led to the collapse of Enron, one of America's largest corporations, and Andersen, the giant accountancy company.

In his book, *The Philosophy of Money*, published in 1912, Georg Simmel wrote: "It is the purchaseability of everything and everybody which involves capitalist society in ever deeper, cynical corruption. The more money becomes the sole centre of interest, the more will honour and truth, talent and virtue, beauty and the healthy mind become a marketable commodity, and a cynical mocking and frivolous attitude will develop towards them. Their value will be considered akin to wares on the street market. The cynical function of money is manifest in its power to transform the higher values into dirty business.

"Everything is marketable, and the value of everything is determined by its marketability, to the point that anything that does not produce profit on the market is not worth anything. This leads to the power of money to seduce people of talent, honour and creativity, who wish to gain recognition and recompense for their labour, into selling themselves to the market. When universal seduction prevails, when those who allowed themselves to be seduced consider the word 'corruption' to be merely an expression of moralistic posturing motivated by envy, it becomes a cultural climate. Then people are resigned to its inevitability as if it were a universal law; indeed, we see that the so-called higher values of truth, beauty and intellectual honesty are considered practically useless, merely self-indulgence: the market is determined by the lowest common denominators of taste and desires which can be most readily manipulated by the advertising industry" (Georg Simmel: *The Philosophy of Money*).

These practitioners of the id justify themselves by a concept of human psychology which can be summed up in the phrase 'human nature being what it is', and we have to take any opportunity to satisfy its impulses. And there are plenty of opportunities.

While it is the task of the ego and the higher areas of the brain to integrate the manifold urges and impulses of the id, its tasks have become undermined by the sheer multitude of opportunities provided by modern capitalism. Our atomised society, split into innumerable segments, has produced an atomised mind, with each of its innumerable parts pushing for expression and demanding attention. But our frantic pursuit of success by whatever means possible does not provide satisfaction for more than the moment. The adrenalin produced in the excitement of making enormous amounts of money does not last long, and we still feel empty.

People who suffer from bulimia stuff themselves with food, until they feel they are bursting, to still their hunger and indeed to ensure that they exist; they have to vomit it out, leaving them with a sense of depression and futility. They feel that the food they devour is unsatisfactory, rubbish, and indeed it is without warmth and love and does not give them the satisfaction they crave for, and the successes they have achieved are ephemeral and meaningless. And this, as I have remarked, applies even more dramatically to prominent artists, entertainers and media personalities who frantically exhibit the good time they are having, feeding the appetites of the masses who emulate the role models of our 'culture': the beauty queens, mannequins, actresses, whose love affairs and marriages make headlines in the popular press and whose pictures fill the pages of colour magazines, whose problems with drug addiction, drunkenness, depressions, disillusionments and various illnesses are unremittingly forced upon our attention. They have it all, but they are left with nothing that matters.

What is perhaps most noticeable is the frenetic-hysterical nature of their exhibitionism, as if they can barely believe their luck of having grasped the opportunities offered by the new freedom and the money to satisfy their greed and vanity. Quick, quick, take it while it lasts now, for if you don't you will be left behind in the race for success and recognition to be seen and admired, you will be lost in the emptiness of an anonymous existence – you would be a nobody. Fashions – outrageous, attention compelling, anything to be noticed to the point of being utterly ridiculous or crazy. Sport – to win at all costs, to be in the limelight and to earn fantastic amounts of money, and to be in the top league.

What used to be called sport, from children's games of mastering and manipulating objects such as marbles and balls, from jumping and skipping and climbing for their own satisfaction as well as receiving approval, to the acquisition of skills of teenagers participating in team competitions and the beauty and pleasure of co-ordinated action of skilled play, has degenerated into the frantic competition to win – frequently aggressive, ruthless and brutal in a mindless competition to win at all costs – not so much for fun and pleasure, but a very serious business in order to be included in top money by being shown on television world-wide and receiving the fees paid by advertisers to promote their product. Businesses invest in sports in order to advertise their commodities on the shirts of the competitors – whether it be football, athletics, cricket – and to display their companies in the stadiums. It is amazing how this is now practically taken for granted and no longer offends people that commercial interests impose themselves upon sporting events. And the spectators – the participants in sporting events who are not actually selected to play – will carry on the fight of their teams in the stands, will shout with violence and aggression in order to make it known that they are also participants in the battle and need to be seen to belong – the professional and the hooligan, the organised fighters and the disorganised fighters. And, if you fight, you prove yourself to be a man, you assert your existence, you are seen and noticed and perhaps admired by women, you are sexy and arouse their desire for you.

Men's Battle to Regain their Masculinity.

This has become important now as men's manliness has taken some heavy knocks and toppled off its traditional pedestal. The breadwinner and fighter in the good old Darwinian model – the battle of survival of the fittest – appears to have become redundant in the new age of over-supply of consumer goods, and the variety of jobs available. In a computer-dominated technology women can do just as well and insist on doing so. The self-assertive, self-supporting, independent women can become the role model in their call for self-realisation. They want to be winners in the battle for the acquisition of wealth and to acquire leading positions in the market-place, with good wages, profits, bonuses and other financial rewards which up to now have been the 'privilege' reserved for men. They are not to be excluded from the jackpots, and the fame which it brings. They defy the old traditions of deference to manliness – they adopt it for themselves.

Men were expected to be rowdy and promiscuous when young, rational and decisive breadwinners until they retired, wise and authoritative and revered thereafter, as Angela Lambert has observed. Feminism reversed all that. It regards men as feckless, over-bearing and selfish – women were saintly and did all the hard work. Women libbers were determined to change both perceptions.

It is interesting that Germaine Greer in *The Female Eunuch* wrote that women's sexuality has been repressed because it served no social or domestic function. She leaves out or ignores the most fundamental dimension of a woman's relationship to men, namely her libido, the urge to be loved and to love, and the pull of sexual desire. She does not acknowledge the woman's own libido as an active partner in their relationship. What happened to her? Has she lost it and projected this loss on women generally, depicting them as mere passive objects of men's desires? What has happened to her erotic passions? How did she come to castrate herself and determine to castrate women generally? She depicts the 'natural woman' as restless, aggressive, unpredictable, provocative and imaginative – indeed, hysterical. Frantically self-assertive, bent upon humiliating the male, insulting them not only in her writings but in her encounters, she is determined to be an example to the modern woman. Of course, there is plenty of evidence for the oppression of women and the denigration of her sexuality in the religions of Christianity as well as Islam.

But why does she herself attempt to denigrate the woman's sexual urges? She gives plenty of evidence in her various auto-biographical sketches by referring to her lost father. He had disappeared from her life and by his disappearance betrayed her love and her need for him, and she is taking her revenge. She influenced a whole generation of women to adopt an attitude of defiance towards men, particularly as many of her militant followers tried to make women believe that the act of penetration is rape. But while women want to assert their masculinity and put an end to penis envy, they also know that they don't really have a penis, and their masculine-sexual as well as narcissistic self-assertion becomes hysterical – impulse-ridden, contradictory and confused, and dogmatic at the same time. Not having a real penis, and having repressed the passions of the vagina, they frequently develop a body penis. (This can also happen with men who are sexually insecure). They eroticise the whole body, swinging their hips in an assertive manner, and enact the assertive drives of the penis in a variety of pseudo-orgastic movements. It is they who make the sexual advances in an assertive and provocative manner, without really knowing what they want, apart from having power over the male. For, after all, they want to receive the penis and absorb it into them, but having repressed their vaginal sensations they feel empty and frustrated. It is natural for a woman to receive a penis, but if she does not receive it, she wants to have one herself.

And when they do get married and manage to assert their equality, and can get good jobs and occupy positions in society on a par with men, their female instincts urge them to have children and to be mothers at the same time. This, as we know, frequently creates conflicts within the home, when they pressure their man to take over many of the activities usually associated with women and themselves feel torn between having to serve the instincts of motherly duties and their determination to participate on an equal footing in what used to be called the men's world. They try to eliminate the biological and psychological differences between the sexes which have developed over millions of years in the life of our species to ensure our survival. All animals show this division of labour, not only mammals but also birds and even reptiles. It not only ensures the survival of the species but also generates the instincts of love and desire for each other, for mutual protection and the care and love for their offspring, and, beyond that, a feeling of community with their tribe. The Darwinian law of survival of the fittest is in no way restricted to the individual but applies to the survival of the family, the tribe and, beyond that, the species. It creates the sense of unity biologically and genetically inscribed in the instincts of all higher animals and made conscious in humans through the capacity of devotion and responsibility. So, in their different ways men and women are united to fulfil their humanity as equals. We must, however, take into consideration that humans are not merely instinct driven, as their mind creates a large variety of fantasies and theories about the destiny and purpose of mankind.

This applies equally to men and women, particularly at a time when the ancient religions and social restrictions imposed upon women are now generally loosened. Women who are endowed with a good intellect will want to use it by being doctors, lawyers, poets, artists, writers, or entrepreneurs. We now understand that it would be wrong to suppress their talent and should encourage it. This may cause conflicts in the woman's mind, as well as in her relationships, and as is well known can frequently cause neurotic anxieties. But if she is sincere and convinced that she wants to devote herself to follow her chosen purpose and ideal, the male in her life should take it into consideration and respect it, if he loves her. There should be a mutually supportive, open and honest discussion between them how they can regulate their lives. She may prefer her chosen career to having children or if she wants to have children to be sure that they can be taken care of and not be deprived of their mother's love and attention.

In my many discussions with professional women who were neurotically torn between motherhood and their career, I used to put it to them that if they want to have children they must understand that the infant needs the full-time attention of the mother for at least the first two years of its life, and that there should be a mutual arrangement for this to be possible, not only for the benefit of the child, but also for her own peace of mind and her relationship with her husband. It should not be too difficult to take an extended child-caring vacation from her professional activities. After the first two years of being with her baby, they can employ a nanny to take the place of the mother to some extent, and also make sure that kindergartens are available to supplement the nanny's care.

The Waning of the Fathers.

In my book *Foundations of Morality* I point out that due to the enormous expansion of the brain and in particular the frontal areas of the cortex, humans are no longer entirely programmed by instincts and need a sense of direction and purpose to their lives. I spoke of foresight and anticipation of the consequences of their actions with the evolution of intelligence, the ability to think and evaluate their actions before they act and make adaptations of behaviour to ensure survival and well-being in changing environments, and the development of moral concepts to integrate and harmonise their relationships with others. Due to the insecurity created by the wide range of possible actions and choices, men have to learn how to behave towards their fellows and to acquire the skills necessary for survival and well-being. Humans need to be taught the meaning and purpose of their life, and from the earliest times our species developed myths and religious beliefs which helped them to understand the world in which they lived and provided rules of conduct, and duties, which they had to follow, and a sense of responsibility for their behaviour.

The grown-up males – the fathers – went out with the troop of young males to teach them and act as role models which the youngsters could imitate and identify with, creating a community of shared skills and co-operation with their fellows, and mutual interdependence in a common pursuit. From the earliest times of their evolution all human communities and tribes had a culture by which they would integrate the manifold impulses into a coherent purpose shared and supported by its members. In various ways this need for a shared culture has created civilisations up to modern times, and the father has remained the transmitter of the common culture and its beliefs, the teacher, together with other adults, to pass on an ever-growing range of skills, not only for the present but also for the future.

But what has happened in our time, and what is happening to the fathers and the sons? We witness a culture where the fathers' ancient role as guides, teachers and examples to the young seems to have got lost in a frantic rush of disconnected events, without much meaning or focus, and the sons have nothing to identify with, leaving them with a feeling of being abandoned by the world around them. They hate the world which has rejected their role as men, as providers, proud of their responsibilities to the community and their power to serve it. They have lost their teachers, their traditions and their sense of purpose in a world which is split into an enormous variety of skills and cultural, artistic and intellectual pursuits. It is just at a time like this that the role of the fathers – to take the sons out into the world and show them what it is like, to encourage their interests and cultivate their talents – has broken down.

The fathers have lost the beliefs which they are meant to communicate, they have lost the vision of God to which they used to refer when they taught their sons of right and wrong and the meaning of life; they have lost the ideals of the Enlightenment, of freedom, justice and equality; they have lost their belief in socialism and human progress by which many had sustained their belief in the future. They have turned away from their own beliefs and their expectations and have nothing to teach their sons; they are failing their sons as their own aspirations have failed them; they have nothing left in their spirit to encourage and guide the spiritual needs of their offspring and are a disappointment to them, failed fathers and leaders trapped in a culture of universal cynicism where nothing can be believed in, nothing is real in a world of lies and pretences. Everything and everybody rushes about and rushes by, quick, quick, and many people, particularly the young, aren't sure what it has all to do with them. Everybody is harassed and pressured in their various pursuits, but there is no substance or meaning for more than the moment, and even these moments are questioned and fail to be satisfying in the absence of an overriding and assured sense of purpose.

Speaking as a father, Matthew Taylor writes: "Despite the emotionally ambitious nature of modern fathering, no amount of structured play will compensate sons for the more troubling messages they are getting from their dads. I worry that we are transmitting a sense of pessimism and uncertainty to our children – the belief that the world is a hostile, difficult place, with no leavening idea of optimism or progress worth pursuing ...

"At the heart of this unease lies the dwindling of belief in fatherhood as a role of transmission: the handing on of progress and tradition. Over the past two decades a very important change has taken place. We no longer believe our children will live in a better world than us ...

"Do the increasing numbers of us working in the dynamic but ephemeral 'knowledge economy' feel we have anything to pass on? ... Increasingly a lot of us can't describe easily what it is we actually do for a living – let alone hope that our kids might want to do something like it ...

"Our loss of confidence in ourselves as parents should provoke us into a more honest debate about the kind of world in which we want to bring up our children and whether we are going about it in the right way." [2]

The problem of boys and young men has been widely described and discussed in learned and other journals. The erosion of the value of masculinity is not merely a manifestation of their self-doubt, but is reinforced by economic and technological changes in our societies. I have spoken of the male's power to protect and support his wife and children. It used to need physical strength and endurance to drive a plough with oxen or horses, to gather the sheaves of corn, to cut the hay and to build haystacks, get up at four o'clock in the morning to get the cows to the shed and milk them and then muck out the shed, to beat the horse-shoes on the anvil and nail them on the horse's hooves. It needed the apprenticeship of boys to be taught by the men to perform these tasks. They had to build monuments to glorify the nation and its gods, endure the back-breaking labours of carrying stones and rocks to build castles and palaces up many storeys and towers to reach heaven and affirm the power and the protection of the ruler of the nation and to protect its citizens.

The industrial revolution of the nineteenth century transformed the modes of production and vastly increased the capacity to produce an ever-growing number of commodities. Workshops became factories and workers had to serve the machines which dominated and directed the productive process. As the machines became more skilled the worker's skills were subservient to the dictates of technological mass-production. The skilled craftsman who earlier ruled the workshop could no longer exercise his skills, as he had to serve the machines which embodied the skills previously vested in the person of the worker. He lost contact with the people who needed his product and became an anonymous entity called 'the workforce' who neither knew the consumer of his product nor the boss who owned the factories. He became a part of the capital of those who owned the machines and the factories as well as the workers whose value is measured by the profits they can produce for the investors, shareholders, directors, managers and executives of the capitalist enterprise. Workers could be made redundant, surplus to requirement and easily replaced from the pool of unemployed should the investors and executives deem it profitable to employ them. All too frequently the ever-growing productive capacity of machinery led to overproduction, economic depression, unemployment and poverty in large areas of the industrial world.

There was a time, particularly during the latter part of the nineteenth century and the early parts of the twentieth century, when many workers – the proletarian masses driven by a growing consciousness of rebellion – joined the socialist movement and could feel themselves in the vanguard of the battle for the just society which will put an end to the dehumanisation of the actual producer and his estrangement from the product of his labours. The socialist movement would dispossess the exploiters, and the workers would receive the just rewards for their work and regain their dignity as persons in the eyes of their fellow men. They would fight for the classless society which would transform the world into a new Utopia. They would tell their sons of a new

and better world they are fighting for, and quote the intellectuals, writers, philosophers and poets who proclaimed the historic mission of the workers of the world. And in the most difficult
times of hardship the sons would respect and admire their father's
fighting spirit and would read the books of the intellectuals and
steep themselves in the future victory of socialism. Many young
men of the middle classes identified with the hopes of a new and
just society, and preached an end to the cruelties and injustices
visited upon so many of their fellow men, and refused to adopt
the arrogance and indifference of their own class. They saw themselves as representatives of the Enlightenment which would sweep
away the worship of power, tyranny and greed and liberate men's
inherent capability to conceive of a just society built upon rational
and moral judgements.

But what has happened? The socialist dream was shattered and
trodden in the dust by dictatorships which in the name of the
workers oppressed and exploited them for their own glorification
and power, surrounding themselves with a body of bureaucrats
who dictated every aspect of life with a ruthlessness not seen since
the Dark Ages. They assumed the right and the duty to kill dis-
senters or torture them in their Gulags, ensuring their gradual
death by starvation and unbearable labours. They provided a
model of mass murder for the tyranny of Nazism whose mind-
boggling crimes against humanity can never be forgotten. Between them they left not only a deep wound in civilisation which
continues to hurt the conscience of Western culture but robbed
the working class of their faith in socialism as the vanguard of
their struggle for the just and humane society. Their historic
mission has collapsed and there is nothing left to struggle for,
no chance of re-establishing their sense of dignity in the pursuit of a better life for all. The fathers have nothing much
left to be proud of and nothing to show and teach their sons.
They have withdrawn from their role as teacher and model and
have nothing to say or discuss, and have disappeared from the
spiritual horizon of their sons. All they can communicate is a
disenchantment and cynical acceptance of the way the world
is, and all one can do is to take things as they are and look
after one's own advantage, try to get a better wage and better

working conditions under the given system, for, after the abortive revolutionary struggles, capitalism is the only system that works, and we have to find a niche within it. Apart from the few who still cling desperately and 'unrealistically' to the old beliefs, the majority of the working class have to submit to the establishment, but occasionally try to get the better of it by a display of trade union power.

The disillusioned fathers, having withdrawn into their compromises and cynicism, have left no spark of fight and rebellion, nothing to be admired by their sons hungry for an image of masculinity. When they look into the water – Narcissus' mirror – to find an image of themselves, they see a picture of anger and revenge – Narcissus denied. They plot for revenge against the world that has no place for them, their faces clenched in a sullen scowl, their eyes hostile, rage pounding incessantly through their skulls and they want to get their own back upon an indifferent world and find a way to make money by plundering and robbing those who seem to have got the better of them. They can't, and don't want to, join the system, but they can make money by terrorising children and older people and rob them of their mobile phones or wrist watches or their cars, mugging people, particularly the old and defenceless for whatever they might get. The satisfaction they derive from attacking, torturing and even all too frequently killing completely innocent strangers, is a driving force for their behaviour, the only way they know to discharge their anger. They want to defeat the rules laid down by the authorities and their enforcers – the police, the school teachers, the social services who are meant to look after them, and the beneficiaries of the system – from the rich and famous to the old ladies collecting their pensions from the post office.

Every day we can read newspaper reports of the endless manifestations of this pathology and all too frequently experience them personally. While they appal and frighten the public, nobody seems to have a clue what one can do about it, apart from possibly increasing the number of police officers, while there is hardly any room left in the overcrowded prisons. Like an infant who bites the breast of an indifferent and apparently hostile mother in order to penetrate her armour, frustrated youngsters are frequently driven by sadistic drives towards an indifferent and un-loving world. The no hope generation can only react to the world by attacking it. These boys find a sense of community by join-ing the violent band of no hopers, creating mayhem and destruc-tion as the only way left to them to assert themselves and find a sense of identity. Violence is the only form of self-expression left to them and they feel good after the most horrendous crimes they have inflicted. Gang rape is a particular way of expressing their sadism towards a rejective or hostile womanhood.

But there is another dimension to this problem: they not only refuse to join society, society itself has made it increasingly dif-ficult for them to join it. Rebelling against all authority, they could not submit to the disciplines of education as demanded by the 'establishment', and could not learn what it had to teach. Their idea of growing up into manhood is to be a rebel, defy-ing any notion of order or submission to school and its teachers. To be ignorant and uneducated became a virtue proclaiming the true character of the rebel. In the end there is no place for them in the economy of the nation and no way for them to earn an honest living: "After eighteen years of Tory rule almost one in five households in Britain has no one in work", as Mr Blair told the House of Commons.

For at least two decades the prevailing wisdom has been in favour of letting failing businesses, especially the heavy indus-tries and smaller firms, go to the wall. As Michael Gove put it in *The Times* 9 August 2001: "The principle of creative destruc-tion, the Darwinian notion that the weakest commercial concerns should not be propped up, for that only saps the strength of the whole economy, has become an almost unchallenged presump-tion. Any lame ducks need strangling, not swaddling."[3] And we might add that this also applies to individuals who do not suc-ceed in the battle for survival in capitalist society; they are left in the outer regions of failure, the wasteland of the useless.

But here is another paradox. The economist and writer Anatole Kaletsky proclaims: "Humanity is starting to enjoy the fruits of boundless economic creativity, because the world has understood how to unleash the power of Adam Smith's profit motive, without succumbing to the political instability and social injustice of the untrammelled capitalist system described by Karl Marx ... The success of the Federal Reserve Board and the Bank of England in protecting the longest business expansion in human history ... clearly represents the economists' finest hour." [4]

In the same issue of *The Times* (28th March 2002), there are two letters in the Letters page under the heading 'A wonderful world?' One is by Catherine M. Castree, who writes: 'Sir, Great Britain is facing growing global insecurity, a hugely rising crime rate, failing health and education services, a transport system in chaos and a postal service near to collapse'; another from Mr Julian Oxley: 'Sir, You say (leading article 25th March) that "on the whole [the world] has changed for the better". Is that a world which is freer from terrorism, conflict, poverty, and man-made environmental damage? ... Are there fewer crimes of violence, shorter hospital waiting lists, smaller school classes, more plentiful and punctual trains, and higher standards of conduct in public life? If so, it is a different world to the one which I inhabit.'

These letters show the contradiction between the view of economists who measure the prosperity and well-being of a country in quantitative, statistical monetarist terms and the actual experience of reality among a very large section of the population. The belief in the single-minded pursuit of profit has led to the decline of traditional industries and to the destruction of long established patterns of employment. In particular, it saw industrial workers thrown out of their jobs in their middle years while new jobs in the growing service sector were taken up by a new generation of the aspiring middle class able to serve the demands of the new economy driven by computer technology, equally available to young men as well as women. The effect on men robbed of their traditional role as providers in the family is shown in the divorce statistics and in the number of young women reluctant to commit themselves to marriage. The increase in the number of children growing up outside wedlock – families without fathers – has risen dramatically in Britain and the United States in the past twenty years. The proportion of births outside marriage is 37% in Great Britain, and it is a fact that children born outside conventional family structures show a much lower level of academic and economic achievement, and their propensity for committing crimes and antisocial behaviour is much higher.

The Invisible Product and the Anonymous Worker.

The computer revolution has to a large extent replaced the traditional manufacturing industry with high-tech electronic information systems, but the skills required do not provide the satisfaction of seeing the product of one's work, there is no physical object which one has produced and which can give a person a sense of identity with the product of his labours. In fact high technology does not produce anything. From where the operator sits, he or she does not see anything coming out of the machine, nothing that is visible and can be touched or handled. All he has to do is to touch keys with his finger tips and assume that this will contribute something to the advantage of his employers who will pay him a decent wage. Computers provide information – information technology – about a variety of purposes, such as where and what to shop, visit restaurants, bookshops, find book titles and authors, beauty and health specialists or the best return for one's savings. It is the chief medium for advertising a vast range of commodities and services – global business at the touch of a button.

Computer technology can design motor cars, ships, aeroplanes, buildings and the machines to produce them. It can program the machines it has designed to make the commodities to be sold and bought – sellers and purchasers brought together in the miraculous circle of computer technology, whose electronic images span the globe with a relentless imperative and abolish all boundaries. But the need to defend the nation from fanatical enemies necessitates strengthening one's defences. And here again computer technology is put at the service of designing and programming rocket systems and a wide range of armaments which create an invincible armoury of defence or attack.

There is simply no time to reflect, to think and trust one's own judgement. There is a profound feeling of harassment among workers in computer-dominated enterprises, and a conscious or unconscious resentment at not being trusted to exercise one's own ideas and skills, which is responsible for the incompetence in many areas of industry, financial operations and government departments.

For a number of years we could observe a process of stupefication in many areas of decision making, a shrinking range of thought, a neglect of the natural function of the intellect which needs some space and some time to function properly to assess the consequences of our decisions, their impact upon our fellow men and upon the world's natural resources. There is an undercurrent of anxiety and confusion, a sense of helplessness in face of the challenge of a world-wide crisis which we seem unable to resolve. We seem unable to conceive of an alternative to the intellectual and moral turpitude in which we are imprisoned.

Many people feel that we are historically at the prelude to mankind's self-destruction and it is at this moment that we need to apply our intellectual and moral resources to their fullest extent: there has to be a vision of a world which makes the future of humanity possible, not only in theory but in reality.

On being in Tune with Nature.

Marx used to say that nature is our body. It is true that nature provides us with the air we breathe, with the sunlight as well as the ozone layer, which protects us from the ultraviolet rays of the sun which would make life as we know it impossible, with water and the organic resources of the planet we need for food. We have to eat, drink and exercise to ensure that heart, lungs, kidneys, liver, stomach, bowels, bladder, the reproductive system and the chemistry of our body operate successfully. In other words, we absorb the resources of nature and its life-giving energy in order to live. We are a part of nature, one of its manifestations, or, as Schopenhauer used to put it, "the individuation of the Will in nature" or, in Einsteinian terms, "of the cosmic energy", and have to keep our symbiosis with nature intact. While health is usually related to the state of our body, the word *sanitas* for 'health' is associated with the 'health of the mind' – sanity, sane.

It is the task of the mind and the collective mind of culture to ensure that individuals as well as communities and nations receive and absorb the life-giving resources of nature to assure a symbiotic interaction between the nature in us and nature around us. We have to re-orientate our responses and create new ways to adjust our ways of living, our expectations and values. We have to re-think the future.

Of course nature herself can have her own disturbances – at least from the point of view of the organisms which depend upon her. There can be climatic changes resulting in droughts or floods, or volcanic eruptions which spread a veil of volcanic dust that cuts out the sunlight and poisons the air. But nature and its organic offspring usually struggle back to create a new equilibrium, making life possible again. Such ecological catastrophes can wipe out many species and at the same time produce new species able to survive. But as Julian Huxley declared, in higher animals and particularly in humans it is the mind which is the agent of evolution.

PART 2 Practical

CHAPTER 4

Liberating People's Creative Potential

The Humanisation of Work.

Man has often been called the animal that produces; he no longer sees himself as part of nature but confronts it as a source of sustenance to provide the food and the raw materials he needs to build shelters, huts, houses and cities and to make tools to facilitate and improve his productive capacity. In the process of work he moulds and changes nature, and he moulds and changes himself in the process.

For hundreds of thousands of years humans were hunter-gatherers transforming stones into tools to reap naturally-grown vegetation and to make weapons to hunt animals. Man was still in tune with nature, he did not transform it but engaged in it as he found it. But with the beginning of agriculture he changed his natural environment, and by his work made it yield its life-giving riches. He separated himself from nature and from his original unity with her, but at the same time he unites himself with her as her master and builder. By moulding nature to his purposes and re-creating her, he learned to make use of his powers, increasing his skill and creativity.

The very success of his tool-making ability to master nature encouraged him to make a growing diversity of tools and acquire the skills to make them, and a wide division of labour emerged, particularly with the development of large settlements and eventually of towns, such as Jericho which brought together a great number of craftsmen with many different skills. It can be assumed that groups of craftsmen working in their workshops owned the tools which they used collectively or, in some cases of a particularly skilled craftsman, individually.

The ever-growing complexity and efficiency of tools produced an increasing variety and quantity of commodities; tools became machines with a growing number of workers to operate them, and workshops became factories. Industrial mass production dominated by machines transformed the craftsman using his tools into a servant of the machine and he became estranged both from the machine and his products. They were no longer a manifestation of his creative work and he had no personal relationship with them. He has become an employee serving the interests of the new owners of the means of production. He is no longer responsible for what he produces, deprived of the exercise of his mental abilities, which are needed to plan the work process and satisfy the public's need and desire for his product.

He is made to ignore the intellectual functions of his brain and the frontal lobes of his cortex are neglected, its neurons 'not fired', as they say, as the worker has lost his sense of being a decision maker in a world that relegates him to be a means to provide the greatest profit for others, who own not only the machines and the workplace but also the worker. He is part of the equipment needed to run mass production industry; its owners ignore the higher faculties of his mind and he is not permitted to activate them. To think about the purpose of his work, how to organise the work process and make the products attractive and available to the greatest number of people who need them, is not what he is employed for. He receives his wages to serve the machines which serve the interests and expectations of his employer, the company, the industrial corporation, the chairman, directors, managers and other experts who know how to run industrial undertakings and to sell products. The worker's ideas on how to run modern industry are not required, he is paid only to do the work for which he is employed.

'Leave it to the experts', is the rule adopted by modern industry, 'they will do the thinking on how to run the business which employs you', and they rob the worker of his sense of responsibility for what he is doing. In fact the 'experts' rob the producer, not only in industry but in most areas of modern life, of the moral and intellectual faculties of his mind. It is no wonder therefore that his faculties of reason and moral judgement atrophy, and it is equally not surprising that consciously or unconsciously he resents this castration of his mental capacities, and he takes his revenge by being indifferent to what he is producing; if he is not appreciated and respected, he cannot respect himself as a producer and cannot respect what he has produced.

A number of political movements emerged during the late nineteenth and early years of the twentieth century determined to raise the consciousness of the workers, such as Communitarian Socialists, Owenists, Syndicalists and Anarchists, who promised that under their social system every person would be an active and responsible participant in the running of social affairs; where work would be enjoyable and meaningful, where capital would not employ labour but labour would employ capital.

They based their hopes for the revolutionary transformation of society on the power and the ability of the working class to overthrow the capitalist system.

The High-Tech Revolution and the Rise of the Service Sector.

In the latter part of the twentieth century a different kind of social revolution has taken place which has dramatically reduced whatever power the working class had in the past, namely the transformation of industry by the growth of computer-dominated forms of production. While previously the machines had become more and more intelligent and skilful than the workers who were reduced to being their servants, the emergence of high-tech computerised industry reduced the size of its work-force and diminished the traditional working class, both in numbers and importance in the economy of the country. The manufacturing sector came to be replaced by the service sector as the major industry in modern capitalist societies. The service sector includes the health services, banking and financial services, the media – such as television and radio, newspapers and journals, the advertising and public relations industry – holiday, travel, hotel and leisure businesses, property management and estate agents, the stock exchange and its breed of dealers and investment advisers, the retail and distribution industry, the popular entertainment industry and the commercialisation of sport.

It seems astonishing how quickly these changes have taken place, and the workers of the traditional manufacturing industries who became surplus to requirement were transferred to the service sector and absorbed in its activities.

The services they provide are taken for granted by the public expecting to receive the benefits without having to make the efforts which were previously required. Governments increasingly see themselves as providers for the welfare state and pass laws on behalf of the social services which are assumed to benefit the public. Thus the government and political parties attempt to get the public to vote for them by political propaganda, while commercial establishments want to increase their sales by advertisements. This causes an ever-growing section of the population to regress to the receiving mode of which I have spoken earlier, which atrophies the giving mode whose ultimate expression lies in the satisfaction of creative activity. In fact, we become deprived of the innate satisfaction of making things happen by exercising our manual or intellectual skills, and also lose our sense of responsibility for what is happening in our environment and in the world in which we live.

We then rely on governments, on business and on computer technology to do the work for us and think for us to solve our problems, and whenever there is a social or an environmental crisis we feel compelled to call upon the services of the omnipotent thinking and producing machines: 'Problems created by technology can be solved by technology' is the refrain one hears whenever someone points to the dangers of an untrammelled reliance upon technological progress.

So let us attempt to regain our human role of being 'causative agents' and encourage our sense of responsibility for what is happening in the world.

CHAPTER 5

The Community of Worker Entrepreneurs.

The workplace is the microcosm of the mode of production prevalent in a society, of its economy and the character of human relationships. The principle of the profit motive determines the role of the workers as means for making a good profit for the entrepreneurs who play a major role in the government's economic policies. The profit motive dominates not only the economic system and social relationships but also the culture and the values of a nation. The reason for investing his capital in the acquisition of factories and employing the workforce is the entrepreneur's expectation that it will increase the value of his investment and the workforce employed will turn out to be profitable. But while the entrepreneur expects his capital investment to multiply, the worker's income remains relatively static and increases only with the rate of inflation or in limited amounts beyond it. Apart from getting his trade unions to demand higher wages or to enforce them by strike action there is little he can do if he wants to keep his job.

It is of course true that a company has to keep the cost of production down by reducing expenditure, and that includes wages, or go bust and the entrepreneur and his investors lose a large part of their money, but the same thing applies to the workers who then lose their jobs and their income. It is also true that entrepreneurship can create new industries and employment and generate new demands for their product. It is therefore the widely-held belief that the entrepreneur, who can foresee the public's demand for new commodities and services and has the courage to create new industries, is the real agent of progress. It is also true that the successful entrepreneur spots technological advances and applies them by investing in factories equipped with the latest technology, resulting in the dramatic increase in the size of business enterprises, industrial corporations and multinational conglomerates which impose their commercial interests and their profit-making obsessions upon the nations of the world, using cheap labour available in the underdeveloped areas. Thus the imperatives of profitability enfold the globe without regard to what happens to the people and to the natural environment: the victory of capitalism across the world trapped in the blinkers of the profit motive.

But still, there is the freedom of choice in the democracies of the West, and we have to choose a system of production and distribution which is geared to the protection of nature and the humanisation of work.

The workplace should enable the workers to relate to their fellows and share a common interest and satisfaction in what they make and how they make it. Therefore its size should be limited at first, in order to create a community feeling and responsibility for what they produce together, enabling them to use their intelligence not only as craftsmen but also as decision makers. Their purpose in work would not be confined to receiving their wages, their work not merely a means to make money for themselves or even more so for their bosses, but a satisfaction in itself. The first step, therefore, is to transform the established mode of production, where a large number of workers are herded together to earn their wages in order to assure the profits of their owners, into worker communities where they can enjoy their innate urges to make things by applying their skills and identify with their products, and also with their community whose members can recognise and appreciate each other as persons.

We all share the narcissistic desire to be appreciated not only for our skills and craftsmanship but also as persons endowed with intelligence to make decisions for the way we want to organise our work. And above all we want to be able to decide how we can best meet the requirements of prospective customers, and be aware of the public's demands. Worker communities will be able to discover what people need or desire, and not try to persuade them to buy useless commodities. In the feeling that their products satisfy the genuine needs of people who appreciate their products, they can identify with each other as friends serving a good cause. There are a great number of commodities which can be produced in workshops by a few 'worker entrepreneurs' or by larger groups in small factories. However, the quest for efficiency would make workers want to acquire the best tools or machinery.

Indeed, modern technology enables a relatively small number of workers to perform complex operations and produce a wide range of commodities, which in the past needed a vast workforce. With the advent of modern technology the productive capacity of each worker is enormously enhanced. Many commodities can be produced in workshops and small factories, both in quantity as well as quality.

We can envisage a large number of workshops providing the commodities needed by the people of their locality and beyond, able to compete with the factories owned by the capitalist corporations. They could be accommodated in residential areas in direct contact with the population, and they would understand their needs. Workshops could be located in houses, blocks of flats, in basements or ground floors. People in the area would have personal contact with the members of the work communities and discuss their requirements in a personal manner. Children would get to know the producers, and discover what they are doing and the way the things they and their parents use are being made. They could be shown how the workshops are run by craftsmen and observe for themselves how the commodities which in the past they just took for granted are made.

Children could see their father at work, admire his skill and be proud of his importance in the workplace; they could identify with him and acquire a sense of purpose and meaning in their lives.

I have a vivid memory of the large gardens in the socialist housing estates of the Vienna of my childhood, with kindergartens, playgrounds, libraries and many workshops where children would watch men at work and were sometimes invited to come inside and feel part of the work process. I have retained after all these years my respect for the workers who produce things and my interest in how things are made.

It is difficult to overestimate the beneficial impact this has upon the sons and daughters, for both boys and girls want to be proud of their dad, for without it they lack a sense of purpose and direction and frequently descend to antisocial and defiant behaviour.

The larger workshops or small factories could be situated outside the densely populated areas, but with easy access to the workers' homes. Such places should be made available by town planners and architects, as I point out later. There is also the question how a number of skilled workers would be able to find each other to form a community of worker entrepreneurs. I shall deal with this question in the chapter on education and skills training. But having found each other, they confront the problem how they can obtain the money to buy their tools and machines and pay for suitable locations for their workshops or factories. While one can assume that they would be able to acquire their tools without outside help, machines would be beyond their means. They could get loans from banks and investment companies, but this would subject them to high rates of interest. Banks and finance houses would want to be assured that their investment is secured by the profitability of the company they help to finance and might want to appoint their representative or director to supervise its activities. This would impose a burden upon the work community and limit its freedom to organise the way its members want to run it.

I suggest therefore that the government creates a Workers' Bank with the specific task of helping worker communities to get started by providing the initial capital outlay with a low rate of interest, without undue financial pressure, to allow them the freedom and the responsibility for running their enterprise.

We are speaking here of a work community of skilled workers and craftsmen, experts in their particular field who share their skills and their enterprise. They would not be subject to the iron laws of capitalism which depends upon the profit motive and the culture of consumerism to ensure the widest possible market for their produce by whatever means their sales experts can dream up without much consideration or care for people's actual needs. A workers' community would in any case be in direct contact with its customers and could easily assess what people want to buy, and organise their production accordingly. They would provide a social service. Above all they would maintain a state of mind and a sense of purpose committed to the needs of the public.

Okay, this is all very well, we might say, working for a local community, but what about modern urban areas with millions of inhabitants who demand large-scale production to provide the things they require. Moreover, fashions can change quickly and people want ready access to the products which they think they want, here and now. It is not always easy to predict correctly the quirks of quick-changing fashions and the market for mass-produced articles. The workers themselves, or at least a group amongst them, would have to keep their eyes open for new fashions and possible demand; they could be assisted by a government sympathetic to the 'new democracy' which would make social scientists available to them with experience in the assessment of the taste and requirements of the public.

The communally-owned factories could organise their products accordingly, as long as their skills and their machines were geared to meet the demands of prospective customers. There is of course an immense variety of commodities which have to be made available: furniture, interior decoration, bathrooms, instant hot and cold water, heating, sanitation, fashionable clothing for men and women, the processing of ready-made foods as well as materials for the building of houses, among others.

Factory production tends to be specialised but this also applies to workshops and small factories which produce certain specific commodities employing workers skilled in those fields. Plumbers, carpenters and tailors do not work in the same workshop nor do they work together in factories. There is, therefore, no technical barrier to the expansion of workers' communities into factories, and they would still be informed and advised about the state of the market for their product. They would also be expected to communicate with other factories, and explore ways of co-operating in the production and sale of a wide range of commodities. For instance, small factories could be subcontracted to supply components for motor cars, railways, aeroplanes, major electrical engineering and many other forms of industrial production. They would also have the opportunity to co-operate with each other and share information about the state of the market. There could be co-operative design centres, for instance, for a transport system which is both aesthetically attractive and efficient. There would also be opportunities for innovation, such as electric motor cars, buses and trains; for renewable energy sources, such as wind turbines, which could be much more energy efficient and less obtrusive, to supply energy for industrial production, as well as solar power to supply lighting and heating for homes.

Thus the spirit of co-operation would free industry from the compulsions of ruthless competition for a largely artificially created market while the basic needs of the public are ignored. While one can assume that the workers' communities would have their own ideas of what people need to improve their lives and to have an intuitive understanding of the prevailing market, nevertheless a more scientifically-based information service would not come amiss to prevent workers from producing commodities which are already in oversupply.

CHAPTER 6

Education and Training

Historical Background.

It is the aim of education to transmit and perpetuate the culture of a society, its moral values and customs, and to teach young people the rules and ideals of their civilisation. During the pre-school years of childhood it is the parents' task to civilise their children and inculcate the values and forms of behaviour expected from them. A society which demands unquestioning obedience and submission to authority will encourage parents to exercise their authority over their children and punish them if they defy their rules and commandments. It is then the duty of parents to instil discipline and obedience in their offspring, so that when they grow up they will submit to the commands of the authorities and recreate the authoritarian character of their culture. The character of a culture is reproduced in a person's upbringing and education, and a person's education in turn reproduces the character of his culture.

Feudal societies educated the young to be in awe of their king and to feel proud to serve him. Their purpose in life was to contribute to the power and glory of the aristocratic establishment.

Of course, aristocratic rule and the propagation of religious beliefs interact, as the power and glory of kings are underpinned by the Church, in order to inspire the people with the eternal verities of God's commands, the creator of the universe and his son, the saviour of mankind from its sins.

The responsibility of education during the feudal aristocracy of the Early Middle Ages was in the hands of the Church. It held the monopoly on learning and literacy, and without clerics to help, even the simplest tasks of government could not be carried out.

The monasteries were the only centres of organised education from the sixth century onwards and dominated intellectual life.

Kingship came to be regarded as a sacred office, with the king more a priest than a tribal ruler. He was God's representative and his supernatural character was symbolised in the ceremony of anointing, marking him off from other men. This transformation is most clearly epitomised in Charlemagne, who in addition to being king of the Franks became at the hands of the pope, emperor of the Holy Roman Empire in AD 800. In government Charlemagne relied upon the Church. It provided the surest means for strengthening and maintaining his empire; his baptism and his bishoprics were the best guarantee of co-ordinating his own tribes into the unity of nationhood.

It is hardly surprising that education and Christian propaganda occupied a leading place in the Carolingian empire. Only through a literate and trained clergy could the empire endure and its objectives succeed. Thus we see a conscious educational policy designed to stimulate learning. From the first, however, it was a Christian one, and it was concerned not with reviving the philosophical speculations of classical times but with training ecclesiastics in knowledge of the Scriptures. Its chief object was an understanding of the established truths found in the Christian Bible and in the writings of the Church Fathers. With the Carolingian empire – the Holy Roman Empire – we have the first great victory and consolidation of Christianity in Europe.

With the crowning of Charlemagne by Pope Leo III on Christmas Day of the year AD 800, the papacy asserted its right to make and unmake emperors, and Christendom became the unity behind the separate Christian states. Thus the figure of Christ, the Saviour of the world majestically enthroned at the centre of the Cross, flanked by the symbols of the evangelists and surrounded by the twelve Apostles, is an image that came to dominate the whole of the Middle Ages, conditioning the world-view of contemporaries as well as their attitude to society and public duty. The search for ultimate truth, like the search for ultimate authority, led back to a single source – the teaching and agony of Christ. It united countless tribes and kingdoms into a community of guilt, with the Church holding the key for redemption. The Cross became a symbol of magic that reminded people not only of their sinful nature but also of their salvation through Christ. It became a shield against innumerable fears and terrors, both psychological and concrete, which had beset men since time immemorial. With the political as well as spiritual victory of the Church, the dogma of man's original sin became firmly established in the consciousness of European man.

By declaring men's sexual urges to be evil, the devil's doing which had to be conquered, the Church gave not only sexual repression a new urgency but also set in motion large-scale regression to pregenital, infantile fantasies. Symbolic representations of archaic fantasies poured into the consciousness of medieval men and populated their universe. Devils, witches, gnomes and monsters, demons of all kinds crowded the imagination of medieval men and found expression in their art and cosmology. A mass of facile beliefs and childish fantasies degraded the ideas of God and reduced even the concept of Christ to primitive magic. According to Gerson, writing in the fourteenth century: "The world is exposed to all sorts of fancies, dreams and illusions, and mysticism is brought into the streets. Many people take to it without suitable direction, indulging in too rigid fasts, too protracted vigils and too abundant tears, all of which disturbs their brains. There is a disorder of the imagination which in its turn is due to diabolical illusion."[1]

Oral-aggressive, sado-masochistic and anal fantasies played a major role in the hysterias of the Middle Ages. "Thus, many saints were conspicuous for their fanatical reverence for virginity, taking the form of a horror of all that relates to sex. Saint Colette is an instance of this. She is a typical representative of what has been called by William James 'the theopathic condition'. Her supersensitivity is extreme. She can endure neither the light nor the heat of fire, only the light of candles. She has an immoderate horror of flies, ants and slugs, and of all dirt and stenches of all kinds. Her abomination of sexual functions inspires her with repugnance for those saints who have passed through the matrimonial state, and leads her to oppose the admission of non-virginal persons to her congregation. The Church has ever praised such a disposition, judging it to be edifying and meritorious."[2]

Oral-aggressive characteristics found expression in the large number of demons and devils. The image of the devouring Christ is vividly described by Ruysbroeck[3] in *The Mirror of Eternal Salvation*: "His hunger is immensely great; he consumes us entirely to the bottom, for he is a greedy glutton with a voracious hunger; he devours even the marrow of our bones ... First he prepares his repast, and in his love he burns up all our sins and our faults. Next, when we are purified and roasted by the fire of love, he opens his mouth like a voracious being who wishes to swallow all."[4]

The Renaissance and the Enlightenment.

Christianity is still nominally one of the leading religions in the world today, but its influence has been greatly diminished particularly among the nations of the Western world both in its power as well as its spiritual message. Indeed, it has no longer any influence upon the political and economic organisation of Western society, which is entirely secularised, even while the churches and their clergy endeavour to uphold their own moral certainties to which a few people cling for the sake of tradition and a sense of belonging in an increasingly complex and confusing world. Education is for all practical purposes in the hands of the secular organisation of the state. There are still a few Catholic kindergartens and schools, but their role in the dissemination of ideas and beliefs about the nature and purpose of life is practically nil. Indeed, the vast majority of people simply ignore the instructions and commands of Christianity, particularly its guilt-ridden paranoia about the sins of the body, and we find an overassertion of sexuality in public as well as in private. The more sex the better is the new commandment, and anybody who considers it to be sinful is mercilessly ridiculed and held to be mentally disturbed.

The spirit of the Enlightenment which has conquered the Western world had its foundations in the European Renaissance which rediscovered and enthusiastically absorbed the philosophy of Athens and its passionate admiration for the intellect. Starved of the love for the human body and the free exercise of the mind by centuries of Christian denial, fifteenth-century Italy absorbed the culture of antiquity and brought forth not only a few exceptional individuals but, as its popular culture, a new blossoming of human creativity which was to become the example for the liberal civilisation of Europe. A new optimism emerged in the minds of men to vanquish the guilt-ridden pessimism of the Middle Ages. One can say that regimes and people's beliefs can be divided between those who are optimistic about human potentialities and those who are pessimistic about men's natural inclinations – liberal or authoritarian, democratic or repressive. Men strove to rehabilitate the body, the senses, the heart and the intelligence, and they rekindled the fascination for nature.

The conception of man's humanity was proclaimed by Pico della Mirandola in his essay *On the Dignity of Man*, which Burckhardt declared to be one of the loftiest of that great age. God, he tells us, made man at the close of creation to know the laws of the universe, to love its beauty, to admire its greatness. He bound him to no fixed place, to no prescribed form of work, and by no iron necessity, but gave him freedom to will and to love. "I have set thee," says the Creator to Adam, "in the midst of the world, that thou mayest the more easily behold and see all that is therein. I created thee a being neither heavenly nor earthly, neither mortal nor immortal only, that thou mightest be free to shape and to overcome thyself. Thou mayest sink into a beast, and be born anew to the divine likeness. The brutes bring from their mother's body what they will carry with them as long as they live; the higher spirits are from the beginning, or soon after, what they will be forever. To thee alone is given a growth and a development depending on thine own free will. Thou bearest in thee the germs of a universal life." [5]

Pico della Mirandola (1463-1494) read Plato in Greek and Moses in Hebrew. When the sacred writings from Jerusalem mingled with the philosophy of the Greeks and were transplanted together upon the soil of fifteenth-century Italy, a new flower grew from it unlike any flower man had seen before.

In his book *Heptaplus*–Discourse on the Sevenfold Narration of the Six Days of Genesis, Pico della Mirandola endeavours to reconcile the *Timaeus* of Plato with the *Book of Genesis*. He dedicated his book to Lorenzo the Magnificent, whose interest in the wisdom of Moses was well known. In proclaiming the harmony between Plato and Moses, Pico imbues every natural object with a higher meaning as an analogue to a divine purpose. Jewish cosmology, governed by a moral purpose, and the Platonic concept of human reason combined to produce an image of man who is not a helpless victim of the cosmic conflict between good and evil, but a being who in his freedom to exercise his innate potentialities is capable of fulfilling God's aim in the world.

In the full exercise of his reason and will-power, the man of the Renaissance not merely attains a sense of his own achievement but through his achievement he also fulfils the design of God. The idea that the full exercise of men's abilities pleases God was perhaps the most significant factor in the maturation of European man. Men ceased to be afraid of their own individuality. The poet of the Renaissance, in setting forth and relating the depth, wealth and variety of individuality, became the most celebrated herald of his time.

To the Athenian, self-rule by discussion, personal responsibility, direct participation in the life of the *polis* at all points, were the breath of life. It is true to say that the Athenian *polis* became an inheritance of European consciousness, an expression of political and personal maturity that served as a model for civilisation but all too often remained an unattainable ideal throughout the subsequent history of Europe.

Athens from about 480 BC to 380 BC was clearly the most civilised society that had yet existed and came to exercise a commanding influence on the consciousness of the Western world, a permanent inspiration for intellectual and moral excellence. It became a kind of collective ego ideal of Western civilisation that strove to replace the older religious superego.

Are beauty and justice innate to the soul and revealed to men spontaneously by intuition or must they be learned? Can the just society be established through love for mankind or by submission to rationally established rules?

This paradox has left European democracy not only puzzled

but in a state of despair in view of the outbursts of barbarism which have overtaken the twentieth century and now threaten to turn the twenty-first century into an insane orgy of destruction the like of which has never been seen before. How could Western democracies, the inheritors of the ideals of Athenian civilisation and the genius of the Renaissance, become overwhelmed by an onslaught of religious and national fanaticism which shows no traces of freedom and liberty? What has gone wrong with the teaching and education intent on communicating these ideals? Freedom, equality and justice assured by laws made by man are the supreme principles upheld in democratic societies, and the greatest thinkers endeavoured in their writings and lectures at universities to convey the message of the Enlightenment.

The great intellectual fighters for mankind's liberation from dogma and authority, David Hume, Immanuel Kant, Adam Smith and, more recently, Karl Popper and Isaiah Berlin were, among many other philosophers since the eighteenth century, the chief protagonists of democracy. Their writings and lectures became the focus of higher education and are referred to whenever social issues are discussed, but many of them declared their reservations about eternal verities. Karl Popper attacked Plato for asserting that the eternal ideas are innate to men's mind and the true guides to the intellect and the conduct of life. He considered that this undermined men's freedom to follow their own ideas and inclinations about their purpose in life. Isaiah Berlin goes to great lengths in discussing liberty and defines it as the freedom from any kind of coercion, but does not dare to ask freedom for what, for what ends and what purposes, because the declaration of a universal purpose shared by all men would inhibit their freedom. Indeed, he follows the philosophical fashion of cultural multiplicity or cultural relativism. Kant was one of the few philosophers who dared to ask this question, and in his work on ethics he arrived at the concept of the Good, the Good Will which is shared by all 'sensate beings'. But this has been attacked by modern philosophers as a metaphysical concept which has no rational or empirical foundation and contradicts observed facts.

In the previous chapter I spoke of the humanisation of work

in the community of intelligent worker entrepreneurs which encourages not only their skills of production but also the exercise of their intellectual faculties and a sense of responsibility for the good of society. To this end we need to educate young people to cultivate their mind and bring out their innate potentials; not only to teach them the way things are and relate to the given reality in which they live, but also to train them to think about the way things should be, to become 'causative agents' for the creation of a good society.

Education for what Purpose?

It is the task of education in a free society to bring forth the often hidden talents of their pupils and to encourage their freedom of self-expression (education – from the Latin *educere* 'to bring forth'). At the same time schools have to transmit to their pupils the skills which their civilisation has acquired, first of all numeracy and literacy – how to count, to read and to write – which are necessary for a person's ability to work and to earn a living. In order to activate the giving mode, a person has to receive the knowledge and the skill which society has to offer. But beyond reading, writing and arithmetic, schools have to transmit and teach a wide range of knowledge concerning the nature of the universe and life on this planet, about evolution, anthropology, history and geography, and the ethical concepts of their culture.

Thus the accumulated knowledge of science and philosophy has to be offered to young people to enlighten and broaden their mind and to discover which particular area of knowledge they feel most interested in. Every human being has the need for a comprehensive image of the world in which he lives, before he commits himself to become a specialist in an area for which he feels a particular attraction.

But there is also a need in every person to make things and to see himself reflected in the things he makes. The urge to create things and transform material objects by the skill of his hands, the use of tools as well as the urge to understand why things are the way they are, is innate to all humans. The way their interests develop depends partly upon genetic endowment and more significantly upon parental and environmental influences and their psychological development. Some of the geniuses of science like Darwin, for instance, were dunces at their schools but developed to become the greatest scientists and discoverers.

Thus the division between work by hand and work by mind is not absolute, and schools have to provide opportunities to develop both aspects of their pupils' potential abilities. Small children should be encouraged by their parents or in kindergartens to experiment with handling things in the form of play, as well as developing their curiosity about the world by listening to fairy stories and all kinds of fables which stimulate the imagination and contain certain basic wisdoms, and encourage their verbal activities by the recitation of poems and singing and dancing together.

At the age of six or so, with the onset of the first puberty when the child has to go out and learn things about the world outside the home, schools have to begin the task of teaching the three basic skills. But even here the child should be enabled to stimulate his sensory activities, such as observation, spatial orientation, listening, speaking and singing.

The first reading books should be interspersed with amusing pictures to arouse and stimulate their imagination and a sense of fun, and contain easily remembered phrases. Recitation of texts stimulates verbal activity and also amusement over the mistakes and errors of their fellow pupils. Counting is to be connected with familiar objects and their relationships.

We must remember that children have a natural need to classify objects according to their similarity and their differences, to arrange them according to their size and shape, to count those which are similar, which belong to one class or another class of objects, or those which a child considers its own or those which belong to others. It would not be possible to collect desired objects and exchange them without the ability to evaluate them according to their desirability. The child must be encouraged to learn to describe their characteristics in words, and he wants his words to be listened to with interest, for otherwise he would regress to infantile modes of self-expression and retard his ability of verbalising his thoughts and his feelings. If he can't express clearly what he wants he has to grab it by force. Or, on the other hand, many children in this situation would withdraw into sullen indifference and refuse to respond to teachers who appear indifferent to them. Thus counting, measuring, verbalising, are instinctual needs which educators must encourage with sympathy to give children the pleasure of actualising and developing their ability to communicate coherently.

The teacher should also be free to articulate his personal opinion about the state of the world, what he thinks about current problems and prejudices, and not hesitate to speak about his ideals and hopes. Such opinions expressed by teachers often have a profound impact upon the child's mind and are remembered as a grown-up.

There is then the question whether children want to become workers by hand or are more inclined towards intellectual occupations. They should wait till they are fourteen or fifteen before making a definite decision. While some traits in their personality emerge at ten or eleven, they may change during their later development. This would mean that all children would be in the same school till they are fourteen, when their choice of profession has become clearer. Having all children attend the same school till they are fourteen would mean that they receive an education which is geared to encourage both aspects of learning, namely the development of manual as well as intellectual skills. All children must have the opportunity to experiment with handicrafts in school workshops as well as receiving some grounding in higher education. A good standard of literacy should be available to all, for instance by acting in classical and modern plays and being informed of the discoveries of modern sciences and what the great philosophers have to say. All the traditional subjects such as history, geography, physics and chemistry among others, as well as politics would be taught and discussed. There would also be instruction in foreign languages, with Latin or Greek as optional subjects. This would eliminate the chronic split between the workers and the educated, with the former consigned to receiving a minimum income when they grow up while the latter's expectation of rewards has no limits.

Teachers should engage children in discussions about what they want to be when they grow up and impart the fact that workers by hand are just as important and valuable citizens as those who are considered intellectuals, each contributing to the welfare of the social community. By the time they are fifteen, the teachers would have a fair idea of their pupils' chief talents and expectations, and the pupils would know what they want to do in life. It is, as I have said before, important therefore that pupils should be encouraged and taught to articulate and verbalise and communicate their feelings and their thoughts.

It is in the interests of society to emphasise and promote the best qualities of its citizens and to show appreciation for their talents, for we know all too well that many people, having their talents unrecognised or being prevented from exercising them, become discontented or hostile, and society loses a great reservoir of abilities to its own detriment.

Those who want to exercise their skills in making material objects, commodities desired or needed by society, must be encouraged to be masters of their trade, to undergo apprenticeship and training in the process of becoming craftsmen. They should not be forced to stay at school longer than they need, for they would come to resent having to be stuck for years in classrooms which they consider alien to their interests, making them restless and frequently rebellious. At the age of about fourteen or fifteen they should enter into the productive environment of workshop or factory as apprentices to learn the skills required of a competent workman and receive a diploma for it, and eventually the title of master of their trade, and, if they wish, start their own company or join a workers' community or become managers of large enterprises.

Every workshop or factory should be obliged to employ apprentices and pay them a certain wage. They should also have the option to enrol in a trade school where they could be trained in their chosen profession. Young people who have the call for more intellectually-oriented activities should stay longer in schools and be prepared for university. No young person should be sent out into the world without a diploma or a degree.

Apprentices would also have the opportunity to acquire some

knowledge of science, philosophy and literature, for which the others are going to be trained more thoroughly, by attending 'Apprentices' academies' one day each week. There should also be popular universities available for adults who wish to pursue their intellectual interests during their spare time without having to become professionals in those areas of knowledge.

One will have to find a suitable name for the schools between fifteen and eighteen which are designed as preparation for university, perhaps 'Further Education Classes'.

At the age of eighteen there would be a grand test of the student's readiness to enter university – matriculation or baccalaureat – and of his maturity to choose –'profess' – his field of learning – 'profession'.

It must be remembered that the word 'university' derives from the concept of the universal – *universitas* – the eternal verities beyond the manifold of phenomena we encounter and observe. In cultures dominated by religious beliefs and certainties God represents the ultimate truth by which the multitude of phenomena are interpreted. He is the *causa prima* and everything that exists is the manifestation of his will and his wisdom. His teachings and his commandments are the secure guide for understanding the meaning of life and the unity of knowledge.

In our modern culture we have broken away from the study of God – *theologia* – as the source of all wisdom and morality, and pride ourselves on having liberated reason and ethics from the shackles of theology. The rational pursuit of knowledge based upon empirical evidence became the guide for the understanding of the universe and of life on this planet. The principle of induction – starting from the study of observable details to arrive at the knowledge of the whole – is the rule for enquiry that merits the name of science.

But the more we learn about the observable phenomena the more they multiply and produce an ever growing number of specialists and experts engrossed in their particular fields of study and becoming compartmentalised in their specialised professions, and there is no room left to arrive at the whole – the core behind the multiplicity of phenomena, to understand the meaning and purpose of life, both of individuals as well as societies. In our society of increasing pluralism and intellectual compartmentalisation we have lost the sense of unity and the interrelation between the many fields of study, each focussed upon its own activity and tending to ignore those outside. This has narrowed people's intellectual horizon in the name of freedom and liberalism and created confusion and insecurity and an egocentric attitude which divides people and leaves them without a sense of common purpose.

Survival of the fittest in a competitive world has become the credo of a misunderstood Darwinism which goes under the name of political Darwinism. Darwin speaks of the survival of the species, and its members are genetically programmed to acquire the skills and the brain power to compete with other species to ensure the survival of their own.

The survival of individuals in the last resort depends upon the survival of their species. And all human beings belong to the same species called humanity, even while there are different races, religions, tribes and nations among them.

It is therefore the task of universities in particular, to enlarge the intellectual horizon of its students by not only making them proficient in whatever field they are interested in but also to consider the purpose of their studies in terms of contributing to the welfare of their community and beyond that of humanity.

There is too much emphasis upon getting a degree for the prestige and monetary rewards it promises. There is an untold number of degrees to be had; many of them have little to do with intellectual excellence and should belong to trade schools. There is nothing wrong with trade schools, as long as they are not called universities.

The investigation and discussion of the *summum bonum*, as well as the meaning of freedom, namely, not only the freedom from restraints imposed by a higher authority but also the freedom to clarify the ends one wants to further should be an important part of university education. The virtues of truth, beauty and justice should not be forgotten.

CHAPTER 7

Architecture and the Built Environment

Some years ago, I gave a series of lectures at the Architectural Association on the crisis of architecture and wrote *A Manifesto of Humanist Architecture* based on those lectures. The students and young architects were enthusiastic about starting an international movement for a humanistic architecture as they had become disenchanted with their profession and many of them had intended to leave it. The older architects were more reserved and tended to resist such a project as they were actively involved and responsible for the designs and the buildings they erected, and they felt that it would harm the prestige and the interests of their profession.

I warned at that time that the homes which they built to house working class people and in particular those whose homes were bombed during the war would become breeding grounds of crime and vandalism, but the profession refused to take much notice, committed as they were to what was then called the engineer's aesthetic or the new brutalism, and chose to ignore the rising criticism of writers and social scientists as well as the public, increasingly worried about the spread of council estates and their aesthetic as well as social vandalism.

But these edifices are still with us and continue to be a blight upon towns and cities, and we now witness an explosion of crime, drug-peddling and violence which makes life on the council estates a torture for those who are compelled to live in them. The 'new brutalism' of the concrete blocks and towers, the actual reality of 'the engineer's aesthetic' which defies all concepts of aesthetics and has no regard for the inhabitants, has created a generation which mirrors the brutality of their buildings. A brutal and mean environment creates a brutal and mean generation which has grown up with it.

There is a historical background to the dehumanising architecture which dates back to the beginning of the 20th century.

The Contemporary Challenge.

Perfection of tools but confusion of aims are characteristic of our time.

Albert Einstein

There can be no doubt that we are confronting a world-wide urban crisis both on the qualitative as well as quantitative level. There is evidence that urban architecture suffers from a deep sense of disillusionment and that in Gropius' words: "We have failed to build the city of the twentieth century which embodies the life of today as an organic whole, because the spiritual confusion of our time has not yet clarified the social prerequisites for its creation." At the same time we confront a population explosion which has vastly increased the number of cities and urban conglomerates. When architecture is faced with the greatest challenge in its history, it appears to be totally unprepared to meet it, being disenchanted with the urban deserts it has created in recent years and confused in its aims.

The modern city is the supreme example of the technosphere getting out of control. Besides the pollution of the biosphere, we must also recognise the pollution of our cultural and psychological conditions of life – the psychosphere.

A Cornell Medical School study of mid-town Manhattan, a mixed but largely prosperous residential district east of Park Avenue with a density of 600 persons per acre, found that "20% of the population were so mentally incapacitated as to be indistinguishable from patients in mental hospitals, a further 60% showed symptoms short of impairment and only 20% were free from the symptoms of mental disease." No doubt extremely high densities play an important part in the production of mental disturbance and neurotic symptoms, as experiments with rats and mice have amply shown. But there are other parameters of psychic disturbance of even greater importance in human beings. The disruption of old established kinship and group relationships play havoc with mind and emotions. The loss of identity, the insecurity in an anonymous human environment, the isolation and loneliness apart from the depressing influences of atmospheric pollution and noise, create a large variety of psychosomatic diseases to an extent that can be called an epidemic.

Urban structures which are dominated by the laws of mechanics and the engineers' aesthetic, largely fail to respond to the biological and psychological needs of man. However perfectly they may express the logic of mechanics they will appear alien to people, they will represent a hostile environment in which man feels himself a stranger forced to live in an emotional void. An organism endowed with mind, intelligence and consciousness needs a sense of familiarity, recognition and empathy with his environment. A purely mechanistic environment that does not respond to his organic and symbolic needs will feel like a prison. A machine for living is a contradiction in terms – one cannot live with a machine. If men became robots, then the machine-orientated architecture could function in a kind of mechanical symbiosis with them. But men are not machines, nor can they ever be, however much they are expected to be in order to adjust to their environment; they are biological and psychological beings and the attempt to confine them to mechanical parameters creates resistance, discontent, neurotic disturbance and epidemics of violence. This no doubt surprises the technological paternalists, but these reactions signify a rebellion, albeit a largely impotent rebellion, against an environment that would not acknowledge the human characteristics of human beings. However, beyond these neurotic and irrational forms of protest there now emerges a more mature reaction.

The Failure of Modern Architecture.

The widespread concern with the technological spoliation of the biosphere is being followed up by the concern with the architectural spoliation of the urban environment. More and more people begin to articulate their revulsion against modern architecture, and in recent years architects themselves have expressed their profound discontent with the edifices they have built or were made to build. An astonishing number of young architects are leaving the profession driven by a sense of disillusion with the prospect of having to build against people. The British House Builders Association declared that the last thing we want to see is a solution like that offered in the 1960s when high rise blocks were seen as a panacea but failed.

Sir Hugh Casson has exclaimed: "The disenchantment with architecture amounts today almost to a kind of paranoia."

We now realise that the love affair with the machine, which has motivated the most influential architects of the 'modern' movements, has created structures which are ugly and offensive. It is one thing to have a design on the drawing-board lit by one's enthusiasm, and another to have it on the ground and live in it. "Both architects and their architecture are disliked by the public ... the old architecture, built up with love and care over many generations, is being thrown away for no good reason."[1] The new brutalism symbolises an indifference to the inhabitants by those who designed and provided the buildings. The Miesian machine aesthetic, as manifest in brutalist architecture, is a slap in the face of ordinary people and can only be explained by the isolation of the architect. He is, as a survey in *The Observer* showed, a typical middle-class man living in the suburbs, keen to escape to the country and keen too on the far more extensive use of plastic, steel and concrete for the town dwellers.

The adoption of brutalist techniques and aesthetics in the massive developments of the 1960s contributed substantially to the feeling that modern architecture was inhuman. "This architecture was damned from the start not only by a sterile boring aesthetic but by its paternalistic authoritarian attitude combined with the blind worship of mass-production and false mechanistic analogies."[2] C. A. Doxiadis has observed: "We have built larger and taller buildings but at the same time we have isolated men inside them. We have limited their lives within this sterilised atmosphere and we have eliminated such natural expression of it as works of art in the open. The age-old love affair between men and buildings is being destroyed in our cities. It is in this environment that civilised man has to live – safe from infections but threatened by degenerative diseases, isolated in the crowd, exposed to neuroses and psychoses. We must face the fact that modern man has failed to build adequate cities. Human forces and mechanical forces are mixed and man is confused ... for man to adapt to our present cities would be a mistake for he is their prisoner." [3]

The protests against the modern architectural environment have not been restricted to 'the man in the street' and a great number of architects, they have been taken up by an increasing number of 'experts of the human condition' – ecologists, sociologists, psychologists, philosophers and poets.

The battle for structuralism, futurism, modernism and the engineers' aesthetic is over. They have failed, and people are baffled as to how to create a new architecture or new parameters and conceptual frameworks to put in place of the old. The awareness of a crisis in architecture is not accompanied by any real knowledge of what can be done to remedy it. What makes the problem of conceiving a new architecture more difficult is the absence of shared values, of a collective imagery by which to define the desirable city. C. A. Doxiadis has written: "I am convinced that the root of all problems in our cities lies in our minds, in our loss of belief in man and in his ability to set goals and to implement them. We can never solve problems and tackle disease unless we conceive the whole. We cannot build a cathedral by carving stones but only by dreaming of it, conceiving it as a whole, developing a systematic approach and then working out the details ... my soul mobilises my whole self into a very positive affirmation: yes, mankind can build the human city." [4]

Let us however remind ourselves that the dreams of the futurists and the functionalists and in particular the fantasies of technological Utopia were largely responsible for the shaping of our modern cities. They had the dreams, a collective imagery of the new city and of the new man which was widely shared at the beginning of the twentieth century. The paradigms of physics, or – more precisely – the popular images of mechanics, became the model from which practitioners in many fields of activity took their direction. If the fantasies of technological Utopia are collapsing all around us, we should not forget that the rigours of mechanistic rules originated in dreams.

The Myth of the Machine.

We who no longer dare to dream, we who have had our dreams stripped of their mystery, should not forget the dreams of our immediate ancestors even if the realisation of their dreams has become our nightmare. But how different and strange seems to us their dream-time long ago – how quaint and ridiculous their credos. Corbusier: "The engineer, inspired by the law of economy and governed by mathematical calculation, puts us in accord with universal law. He achieves harmony. A great epoch has begun. There exists a new spirit. There exists a mass of work conceived in the new spirit. It is to be met particularly in industrial production. Architecture is stifled by custom. The 'styles' are a lie. We must create the mass-production spirit, the spirit of constructing mass-production houses, healthy and beautiful in the same way that the working tools and instruments which accompany our existence are beautiful." His ideal is the house as a machine.

The ideology of the machine that inspires the man who has never worked in a factory is also the idealisation of power, order, regulated lines and mechanical correlations. "The regulating line is a guarantee against wilfulness and brings satisfaction to the understanding." The idealisation of the purity of mechanistic structures is related to puritan taboos upon spontaneous behaviour: "Demand an adjoining room to be a dressing-room in which you can dress and undress. Never undress in your bedroom. It is not a clean thing to do and makes the room horribly untidy" (Corbusier).

It may not be surprising that the first image builders of the machine age, the young Italian futurists Marinetti and Sant'Elia were the harbingers of Fascism. Marinetti's enthusiasm for the new age: "We declare that the splendours of the world have been enriched by a new beauty – the beauty of speed. A racing car

97

with its bonnet draped with exhaust-pipes like fire-breathing serpents – a roaring racing car rattling along like a machine gun, is more beautiful than the Winged Victory of Samothrace. We will sing of the stirring of great crowds – workers, pleasure-seekers, rioters – and the confused sea of colour and sound as revolution sweeps through a modern metropolis. We will sing the midnight fervour of arsenals and shipyards blazing with electric moons, insatiable stations swallowing the smoking serpents of their trains, factories hung from the clouds by the twisted threads of their smoke, bridges flashing like knives in the sun – giant gymnasts that leap over rivers – adventurous steamers that scent the horizon, deep-chested locomotives that paw the ground with their wheels like stallions harnessed with steel tubing and the easy flight of aeroplanes, their propellers beating the wind like banners, with a sound like the applause of a mighty crowd. These men enjoy, in short, a life of power between walls of iron or crystal; they have furniture of steel, twenty times lighter and cheaper than ours." [5]

The will to power vicariously experienced through the machine expresses itself in a new romanticism which, combined with the worship of order and purity, was to find its apotheosis in the spirit of totalitarianism. The power of the machine was further extolled by Sant'Elia: "We must invent and rebuild *ex novo* our modern city like an immense and tumultuous shipyard, active, mobile and everywhere dynamic, and the modern building like a gigantic machine ... The house of cement, iron and glass, without carved or painted ornament, rich only in the inherent beauty of its lines and modelling, extraordinarily brutish in its mechanical simplicity, as big as needs dictate and not merely as zoning rules permit, must rise from the brink of a tumultuous abyss; the street which itself will no longer lie like a doormat at the level of the thresholds, but plunge storeys deep into the earth, gathering up the traffic of the metropolis connected for necessary transfers to metal cat-walks and high-speed conveyor belts." [6]

A new age and a new man was to emerge freed from the encumbrances of a spirituality and symbolic ornamentation that had no significance in the framework of scientific thinking. But let us remember that the purity of mechanics and the powers of the machine are themselves symbolic constructs. The dreams of power may turn into a reality of helplessness and anxiety, and the paradigms of purity and cleanliness become vistas of dirt, pollution and confusion. What is the reality of the dream of mass-transportation and speed? Peter Hall describes it in this way: "These motorways, sometimes elevated, sometimes depressed in trenches, are being constructed through the most amazing scenes of devastation ever witnessed by the people of England. The Luftwaffe never achieved anything like it. The nearest parallel is Dresden, or even Hiroshima in 1945. In the great cities of the north whole areas have been razed to the ground as far as the eye can see. At most a few pubs survive as a sentimental concession to the past. Though not all cities are the same, in many of them the new landscape that is put on this blank map is the same. Huge industrialised blocks up to 20, 30 or 40 storeys high tower into skies" (Peter Hall: *New Society*, October 1968).[7]

But the architecture of the early part of the twentieth century continues to make itself felt in our own time and imposes its image upon our cities as symbols of the architect's vanity. A prominent example is the British architect, Norman Foster:

Behind Norman Foster's towering domination of British architecture lies a man ill at ease with human reality. His buildings clad the establishment in slick modernist clothes, serving power not people.

... He has achieved a near-monopoly of the monuments of millennial London – enough to constitute a city in themselves – designing such essential urban objects as the city hall, two skyscrapers, the bridge, the football stadium, the town square, the train station and the headquarters of a supermarket chain (as well as hectares of office space and flats). And this is to say nothing of the icons and airports he has bestowed on Hong Kong, Berlin, Barcelona, Nîmes, Frankfurt, Tokyo, Singapore, Glasgow, Cambridge and Omaha, Nebraska. Few if any living Britons have the international stature in their fields that Foster has in his.

There is a pattern here. Brilliance and invention are applied to aerial things, to the abstract rules of structural engineering, to places beyond inhabitation. At ground level, in the zone of complex human activity, the design resorts to generalities and platitudes. So here's a hypothesis: Foster is popular because he supplies the look of innovation without the pain of actually changing anything; the establishment likes him because he lets it feel daring at minimal emotional expense; he is the purveyor of radical architecture for people who want no such thing.

To evade challenge, the pillars of English life need to appear as if they are changing. Where Prince Charles failed to win the country over to conservative architecture, Foster has succeeded by giving it a different cladding.

...

His hero is Buckminster Fuller, the American who invented the geodesic dome, an ultra-light structure which (so the fantasy went) could be shipped by helicopter to provide instant shelter. Fuller's other fantasy was that giant domes could cover much of Manhattan, creating immense, climate-controlled zones. Foster took up the idea. "Vast areas will be enclosed with lightweight, space-frame structures or inflatable plastic membranes," he said in 1969. "Full climatic control is feasible; the polar regions can be tropicalised and desert areas cooled."

... The presence of people in Foster's plans is often represented as myriad dots gathering at critical points like iron filings round a magnet. Or else they merge into arrows denoting movement, identical to the arrows denoting air flows in Foster's diagrams of ventilation systems ...

There are dreams here of escape, of purity and of control. They are beautiful dreams with a sinister potential...

He's not concerned with how the building works, but how it looks ...

The old chestnut that transparency equals democracy is offered, even though the GLA's convex form means that the glass reflects the sky, making it opaque. Its bulbous shape is deflective rather than inviting, and is lifted, in Foster's style, off the ground. Little thought has been given to interaction between the public, their representatives and the press. Rather than engage with the building's purpose and its complex site, the architecture is dictated by its look and low-energy design. Foster is thinking global (about CO_2 emissions) but not deigning to act local.[8]

What appears to Foster and to the public as 'innovation' is in fact a rehash of the designs and plans for the 'new architecture' of the early twentieth century.

The parameters of engineering and technology which apply

to the environment are also related to the economic system of society.

The widespread and ruthless use of mass-production engineering, the lack of concern for human beings and the brutalism of structures relate to the profit motive as much as to the requirements of engineering. The capitalist profit motive has created a state of alienation among those who produce the environment as well as those who live in it. By alienation we understand man's estrangement from his own work activity and from the product of his work, from his humanity and the environment which he has created. Both the work activity as well as the product of his work do not belong to him but to the entrepreneur. Both are part of the entrepreneur's capital, a commodity for profit. What they produce are not ends in themselves seen as human creations, but merely the means to satisfy the requirements of capital investment. In the case of architecture the buildings are commodities, articles of investment that must produce a sufficient return on capital.

The architect in such a society takes it for granted that he must satisfy the requirements of the developer. He himself is merely a worker employed by the property owner, and his skill is merely a means to create the greatest possible profit in order to justify the entrepreneur's investment. No wonder it has been said that the most successful architects are those who understand property value and the mechanics of property development. It is widely accepted that the requirements of the property speculator make it impossible for architects to do justice to their skills and aspirations. Disenchantment is also felt by many architects themselves, who find they are being subjected to the demands of the property operator. The work which they do is controlled by men who have little understanding, or interest in the aspirations of architects to satisfy human needs. The property manipulators do not wish to understand the relationship between physical space and the social and cultural communities of the people who live in them. For the developer all physical space is capital. The dependency of councils and local authorities upon market values of land, and the banal mentality of bureaucrats, have been repeatedly pointed out in recent years.

Many people think that the abolition of capitalist market forces would enable architects to create according to their real abilities and transform the destructive and barren technological landscape into worthy human habitations. However, our experience with the bureaucratic mind and with so-called socialist systems dominated by a bureaucratic totalitarianism does not justify this hope. The politics of bureaucracy can be just as deadening as the politics of capitalist manipulation.

The widespread awareness of an architectural crisis and a great fund of good intentions is not enough to pull architecture out of its contemporary impasse and squalor. A conscious awareness of man's biological and psychological needs is necessary for the creation of a humanistic architecture, and in the following pages I shall indicate some of the basic principles which govern human responses to the built environment.

Human Needs Significant to Architecture.

1. The Symbolism of Architectural Form.

Symbolisation processes play an important part in the psychic activities of man. A symbol converts emotions, drives and urges into forms recognisable to the senses; it is the transformation of emotional processes into visual or auditory form. In other words, every emotion subjectively experienced seeks its objective representation. Every culture has its own dominant symbols manifested in its language, mythology, its art and architecture.

Material objects, their feel and their shapes, symbolise emotional attitudes; they mirror emotive states of our own bodies. In every object shape we see a body expressing certain feelings, from the sensuality of a round, smooth pebble that caresses our palm to the heaven-soaring spire and the upward-yearning arches of a cathedral. In the artefacts we build we express both a utilitarian function – a means for satisfaction of biological needs – as well as a state of mind which is spiritually and psychologically important to us. We express dominant psychological drives not only in behaviour and action but also in their symbolic representation in auditory structures like music, linguistic structures like litera-

102

ture and poetry, and visional structures like painting, sculpture and architecture. All these manifest both the psychic preoccupation of the creator as well as the common psychic pursuit of a culture which constantly tries to represent itself by means of symbols. The representation of often unconscious psychic processes in symbolic terms has the purpose of making private and often hidden states of mind public in order to be shared and accepted by the community. The public catharsis of emotional drives and conflicts, the acknowledgement of what goes on unrecognised in the private soul, serves to give acceptance and discharge to otherwise blocked emotions: it is a public communion of deep and often secret desires and longings.

But public symbols of private emotions also acquire a prescriptive or moral significance – they influence the mind and the spirit of the community. Emotive statements once accepted by the community as shared values acquire prescriptive characteristics. They acquire a built-in programme which tends to direct or coerce behaviour. Thus our built environment does not only speak to us in symbolic language evoking emotional responses, it also influences our attitudes and directs our minds. One can say, therefore, that every building to some extent propagates certain values or attitudes – it is a piece of propaganda. Whether we know it or not, our emotional and intellectual orientations are thus influenced by our environment and, above all, by the built environment of architecture.

As we have seen, human beings recreate themselves in their objects. Buildings have bones, skin, eyes, mouths, lungs and heads. The human body is not merely a physio-biological system but a psychosomatic unity. Practically every part of the body, every limb and even the organs are influenced by unconscious emotions, fears and desires. In fact, the behaviour of a muscle or the posture of a limb is related to a person's character, his inhibitions, traumas and emotional attitudes. The sinews of the body are given particular prominence in modern architecture by the steel girders which strut assertively, holding the building together in a state of tension which replicates the body of modern man, who tenses his sinews to control his insecurity and apprehensions of some catastrophe to come.

A few hours after I wrote this, the *Evening Standard*, June 17th 2003, had large headlines on its front page: 'MI5 BOSS: TERROR BOMB IS CERTAIN – NEW NUCLEAR, BIOLOGICAL OR CHEMICAL ATTACK ALERT'.[9]

Just as our emotions find rich and varied expression in the movements and postures of our bodies, so we associate the shape, form and texture of material objects with certain emotions, as if every form adopted by an object were to express a feeling or an intention. This communication between ourselves and objects around us is always there, even though we have long ceased to be conscious of it. The animistic disposition, the heritage of a very ancient cultural development is still with us. We still see a spirit in the things that surround us; even if we are no longer conscious of the messages which objects communicate to us we experience them in our daily lives, and they influence us profoundly.

Architectural forms, therefore, symbolise emotional experiences. They can be aggressive, over-bearing, arrogant, complacent; they can be blind, indifferent, protective or rejective, or give expression to prevailing anxieties.

It is well known that colour evokes strong emotive responses and that certain colours are exciting, pleasurable and elating, whereas others are depressing, gloomy or even anxiety-arousing.

Whereas the body as a whole displays a very wide range of emotional and mental states both in its movements as well as its posture, it is the face which most clearly and powerfully expresses the emotions of man. In the face we can consciously recognise the play of emotions. Upon encountering another person we instinctively look at his face to inform ourselves of his attitudes to us, to learn of his character and his disposition. In a building we see a body that expresses an attitude as well as a face, which mirrors its soul. Upon perceiving a building we instinctively look for its face as if it were an animate being and, especially, we look at its eyes. The building looks at us through its eyes, and in its eyes most particularly we discern its attitude to us. We see the eyes in the windows – windows are the eyes of a building, windows of the soul – and our first attention is focussed on them. Eyes can look at us wide open, trusting, interested, loving, or they can squint in a doubtful, distrustful way; they can look confused and without recognition; they can stare coldly with deliberate indifference.

It is our desire that eyes should look at us with recognition; that they register our presence and manifest goodwill towards us. Such eyes will be fairly wide open without glaring; they will be direct as well as soft; they will be clear, so that we can see ourselves reflected in them; the muscles around the eyes will be relaxed; the eyebrows will share in the inviting posture of the eyes – they will partake in the open, inviting attitudes without a defensive or hostile frown or a withdrawn indifference.

The themes expressed in the face are taken over and orchestrated, as it were, by the whole body. The upward-reaching arms that point towards heaven express the gesture of Gothic transcendence, the suffering or salvation of the world beyond. By contrast, upward-reaching structures may stand with the tight limbs and rigid shoulders of the powerful barons of the Renaissance, or the anonymous and faceless tower blocks which rape the contemporary environment, asserting impertinently and brutally their power over the town. It is indeed a peculiar dilemma of modern man that he not only confronts these symbols of power, but has to live in them. He is completely absorbed by the self-assertive and ruthless representations of his establishment, finding it peculiarly difficult to oppose them.

Huge, blank walls curtaining high buildings direct their eyeless gaze at us, showing an indifference and a non-acceptance under which we cower. Rows of windows that are not focussed by spaces between them create a confusion of glances on which we are unable to focus or recognise an attitude or character. It is not possible to rest one's eyes on them to experience a sense of communication. The glass towers without eyes indicate emptiness – indifference without recognition.

2. The Symbolism of Scale.

The scale of buildings, height and size, indicates their importance in hierarchic relationships. Size is above all symbolic. In ancient towns, the edifices devoted to ritual and religious worship not only occupied the centre of the town, indicating their importance as a psychological focus, but very soon acquired predominance in size and height, visually dominating the landscape. The height of ritual structures indicated the highness of the divinity – it forced men to raise their eyes upwards towards the Higher Being, thereby adopting an attitude of submissiveness. The raising of the eyes is a very important gesture of adoration, submission and humility. And these gestures were originally reserved for the divinity which governed a culture. The fusion of the god Ra with the spirit of the pharaohs in Egyptian theocracy was clearly manifested in the pyramids – one can say that the massive technology and wealth displayed by them combined the power of the temporal world with that of the everlasting spirit of the gods.

The size and height of the pyramids indicate the importance of the spirit buried in it, its importance being perpetuated by the visual power it exercised on the citizens. Thus such structures represent a built-in programme of adoration and submissiveness. As long as these structures represent a meaningful deity to which the inhabitants relate, it serves their psychological needs and reflects upon their own sense of importance.

Even the high chimneys of the industrial revolution symbolised power and progress and thus appeared meaningful to the population. The American skyscrapers can be considered as the cathedral of technology, reflecting a sense of pride in the achievements of American society and its power. Recently the building of ever taller skyscrapers has come to show the technical and economic progress of countries capable of building them. "New York and Chicago have been overtaken by Asia and the Pacific rim. China alone has 22 of the world's tallest buildings. In the past ten years Pudong, Shanghai's new business district has gained a silhouette that took 50 years to achieve in New York and 30 in Hong Kong." This without doubt shows the new spirit of enterprise and technological advance achieved by China which it can be proud of, bestowing its major cities with a new glamour. "While skyscrapers are easily glamourised", and claimed to be the solution to the population explosion, in cities like "Hong Kong and Shanghai, tower housing (as in Britain) has too often been an escape from one slum to another. The massed ranks of 'harmony towers' built by the Hong Kong Housing Authority are a modern hell on earth with 2000 people in each 38-storey block, most with views of nothing but blocks identical to their own." And there are the dangers of "packing people so closely together in an age of epidemics, particularly when sanitation has not been properly addressed" (Marcus Binney, Architecture Correspondent, *The Times*, 31 May 2003).[10]

The anonymous, spiritually neutral, high-rise blocks, which signify nothing but the need to house as many people as possible appear hostile and oppressive. We have to raise our eyes to them and see nothing but necessity – the squalor of a proletariat treated like battery hens or the mindless efficiency of bureaucratic control, coupled with the vanity of architects who want to display their genius.

Buildings in a civilian environment should not reach a height which dramatically exceeds the human scale. They should relate to man without enforcing submissive attitudes. Such scale may be assessed fairly easily in an equation that relates horizontal distance to vertical height in such a manner as not to enforce constant visual submission. Tower blocks should be some distance away from main roads and densely populated urban centres, and should be painted in warm and welcoming colours and have mural decorations. In the hierarchy of values upheld by individuals as well as societies, status and social importance is manifest in the size of buildings and the space they occupy. They also enhance the status consciousness of the population nearby, and act as living museums to show what human ingenuity, wealth and art is capable of, while an environment dominated by nondescript bulky blocks of flats only glorify the commonplace and the prevalence of poverty. As such their very bulk is depressing. They confine people within the necessity of poverty, shutting out any sense of an alternative. No wonder that the large anonymous blocks of flats of the 'new towns' in Britain (those monuments to unredeemed necessity) create an exodus of young people to the bright lights of the capital, and engender a deadening and neurotic depressiveness among the elders.

3. The Symbolism of Architectural Space

The first furrow with a plough – a field. Space comes into being.

Urban constructions are artificial demarcations of an habitation area. Demarcation areas existed long before urban or even village architecture. They depended upon natural demarcations and on the power available to man which determined the range of his movements. The greater the power of his tools and weapons and his totem magic, the greater his territorial range. Territorial definition through demarcation provides kinship identity, property protection and security. Demarcation keeps outsiders out and kinsmen in. Generally the two functions coincide. The defence against extra-territorial threat enhances intra-territorial identity. However, when extra-territorial threat disappears and boundaries remain, they are quite often felt to be coercive insofar as they keep sections of the population within a limited area in order to control or dominate them. Control or domination in our time is mostly economic even though political control and surveillance has increased in totalitarian countries.

The urban grid, which basically represents the military planning of Roman garrisons, became prevalent again in eighteenth century town planning, where it represents a combination of autocratic discipline with the regimentation of the working class. It was employed particularly in the nineteenth century to house the masses of industrial workers, and continues in our time. The architectural spaces of industrial towns reflect the forces of social and economic necessity.

The demarcations of nature and spaces facilitating human association are on the other hand enhancing or liberating spaces. They surround the individual with a sense of familiarity and security, freeing him from a sense of isolation, they affirm his territorial sense of identity and thereby define his personality. In the urban context restrictive enclosures have an angular, geometrically compulsive form, whereas expansive, enhancing enclosures often have an ordered yet ornamental form. They will contain spatial decoration giving scope to curiosity and discovery. Compare the enclosures of Renaissance Florence, Milan and Rome with the working-class enclosures of nineteenth century Nottingham or twentieth century new towns. Such enclosures tend to be empty of sensory stimulation and surround people with a sense of void.

Sensory Deprivation.
There are certain features in modern architecture which create a form of sensory deprivation particularly in children, producing a generation of intellectually underdeveloped people. This is not merely a fanciful hypothesis but has been forcefully underlined in tests with children from new estates and especially tower blocks who have been found to be significantly on a lower intellectual scale than others. One of the most important stimulants for intellectual growth is curiosity and the exploratory drive. We must realise that our senses do not merely receive impressions, that our eyes do not merely register what we see, but we look, and our senses reach outwards towards stimuli and we are driven to investigate and explore. The exploratory drive keeps the brain progressive for it creates new associations by introducing new variations and prevents it from degradation into automatic functions. Curiosity breaks up assemblies of ideas before they harden and re-arranges them into new patterns.

The habit of exploration creates a readiness for higher associations – to explore is to tolerate uncertainty, to accept adventures of the mind, of the unknown emerging into consciousness. It encourages trial and error experimentation with concepts, and activates the higher cortical functions. Curiosity is not only visual, however; it implies the urge to handle objects and discover their uses, to experiment with them, to find out their potential and to discover new uses, to dismantle things and re-arrange them, to break up given material patterns in order to make new material associations and patterns. The stimulus to the intelligence of variability in the environment, the discovery of the unexpected and the need for the mind to find new solutions and answers is of great importance, particularly for children. An environment consisting of ready-made objects with which one cannot experiment, whose uses are pre-determined and not variable, is a disincentive to intellectual growth. The mass-produced objects of the modern environment whose uses are rigid and one-dimensional, as it were, atrophy the co-ordinating associative curiosity of the intellect. The objects whose uses are completely predetermined by industrial mass-production do not stimulate the child into creating new co-ordinates and problem-solving situations, but encourage rigid patterns of mind, intolerance, uncertainty and fear of intellectual enquiry.

In human beings intelligence does not signify merely the adjustment of behaviour to more or less fixed environments but the opportunity for moulding and manipulating the environment into new forms and associations. Intellectual freedom means the availability of a wide variety of courses and patterns to choose from.

The mechanistic, pre-manufactured environment of the home, the mechanical patterns and ready-made objects predetermined by choices made by others – the experts – restrict the scope for creative manipulation. Courtyards and patios are replaced by concrete corridors and tunnels connected by elevators. The concrete playground and the factory-made structures evoke stereotype responses promising no mysteries and nothing unexpected to be discovered. A disposition to a rigidity of mind, inhibition of spontaneous curiosity and fear of the unfamiliar will emerge. It may perhaps be no exaggeration to say that the factory-produced environment creates intellectually and emotionally deprived morons.

The City as a Symbol of Man.
In the modern towns of democratic societies we see the 'free' worker who can offer his labour power on the labour market and who is not committed to any particular employer, without social commitment in his tower block, relating to no one and belonging nowhere. He lives suspended in a slab, without any territorial patterns and without any focus. Each slab stands side by side with no recognisable meaning to them.

The city, on the other hand, is like a woman that gathers her children unto her, surrounded by the magic circle which gives security, identity and a sense of belonging.

The modern freedom from ritual worship, from church and God, has not provided the modern city with an alternative symbolic image. Fundamentally, the traditional city was a sanctified habitation whose identity was derived from the deity to whom it was dedicated. The city of God (and every city aspired to be a city of God, or of a god) must be replaced by the city of man – a city that is not merely for man but which derives its image from man. The human city could be seen as an organic entity analogous to that of a human body having a great number of specialised centres and cellular functions. In biological functionalism each organ and each cell represents a specialised entity yet contains in itself duplication of all the other cells in the body. Each cell, although a specialist, also contains in miniature the characteristics and specialities of all the other cells. Thus, no cell is merely a specialist, no function so specialised that it cannot in some basic manner also perform the functions of all the others.

So it would be with the structure of the organic city. The city, seen as a body, has a head, heart, lungs, stomach, arteries, muscles and limbs. It represents man's needs, aspirations, desires, intellectual and artistic pursuits and political ambitions. In the human city no sector would be completely specialised and isolated from others – each would also contain the manifold interests of all the others in some degree. No man would be merely a member of his social class – he would partake in a wide range of activities and interests that signify a full human being. The co-ordination of individual and communally shared multiplicity would be a necessary and desirable aspect of an organic city. There would be a clearly recognisable hierarchic structure, but this structure would be suffused by interconnecting and duplicating functions spread across the town.

The head, as the intellectual, political and administrative centre would be clearly recognisable in the centre of the town: university and high schools, legislative, administrative and juridical edifices, museums, industrial and business headquarters, theatres, concert halls, library, cathedral, high fashion, cafes, restaurants and entertainment would represent head and heart of the city. In this area there would also be a host of other functions and activities duplicating other areas of the organism, thus avoiding an arid formalism as we find in many towns.

Parks and recreation grounds, swimming pools and sports

grounds would provide the lungs, and some of the muscular discharge for the city's energies.

Markets, restaurants, cafes, pubs, and shops of all kinds would spread across the residential areas, bringing food and sociability into all districts.

Residential areas would not be transit dormitories where people spend much of their time travelling to work or places of entertainment. They would be communities which include production as well as cultural facilities in which inhabitants would partake.

Urban buildings would symbolise territorial identity, with their own gardens and courtyards which are not just open spaces but provide amenities for communal activities and contain kindergartens, libraries, clinics, playrooms and gymnasia. Open spaces should be partly enclosed to give a sense of territorial identity and focus, and provide local activities to satisfy the day to day demands for entertainment and creative activity in which all can participate.

Shops, local industry would all intermingle in courtyards and streets; families would not be isolated from the community, work territory not isolated from living territory, leisure not isolated from productive creativity. The overt display of interests and talents in communal activities directly connected with the habitation stimulates vitality, sociability and friendship.

People who live in modern cities are surrounded by thousands of people yet nevertheless often feel isolated and lonely. A few are physically lonely – most live in a state of inner loneliness. There are thousands of encounters, but these encounters are ephemeral and unsatisfying. The increase in mobility, speed and casualness of relationships causes a defensive attitude where people do not wish to expose their inner being and are thus left uncommitted to each other, often seeking gratification in fantasy life or in organised, impersonal entertainment provided by the media and television watching. The triviality of the majority of human encounters is accompanied by that sense of anomie of which Durkheim has spoken – that sense of alienation of man from his environment which is one of the most damning aspects of modern society.

One of the reasons for this malaise, now widely recognised, is the inability of urban areas (which falsely call themselves cities) to provide the physical and symbolic setting for the manifold social needs of man: their failure to facilitate intimate contacts between people.

The satisfaction of the social and psychological needs of people would be the chief aim in planning and building a city. The building of such a city is no longer merely a luxury – it is becoming a necessity at a time when building on a very large scale must take the place of piecemeal, chaotic planning, and the image of the human city must guide architecture.

It is important that we have a vision of the healthy and life-affirming environment to which architects can aspire, and an understanding of people's needs. The following five human needs should be satisfied by a humanistic architecture:

the need
1) to feel respected and acknowledged as persons;
2) to experience a sense of community;
3) to provide a diversity of stimulation, encourage curiosity and discovery in a feeling of unity in diversity;
4) to satisfy the desire for beauty and aesthetic values;
5) to encourage a sense of pride of belonging to an environment which its inhabitants can admire and identify with.

We may call these the five principles to which a humanistic architecture should aspire.

CHAPTER 8

What Do We Mean By Democracy?

I have spoken earlier of the experiences of the embryo, the impact of its mother's attitudes towards it and the child's post-natal development of a sense of self, its narcissistic needs to receive love, affection and attention, to feel love in order to love itself and to give love and recognition to others. I spoke of the receiving mode and the giving mode in the development of a person's character, and we can extend such qualities to the character of a society. A good society will give sustenance and recognition to the physical and emotional needs of its members and share its accumulated knowledge and wisdom with them, encourage the development of their minds, invoke their curiosity and show what it stands for, its ideals and purposes, so that people can receive, absorb and judge its values. A healthy and confident culture wants to embrace its members and respect them as persons, listen to their opinions, and value their contributions to society.

It has been said that there are fundamentally two types of cultures: those which are optimistic about mankind and those which are pessimistic. The latter considers it necessary to repress people's sinful, anti-social and destructive drives by making them feel guilty and imposing strict controls and taboos through the rule of a superior élite, such as an aristocracy or dictatorship, the unquestioning submission to the dictates of a religious belief or in our time a ruling class which upholds the eternal values of market forces and wants to extend its rule over the world as a global market.

But what is the alternative? We are trapped in our acquisitive culture and pressurised into buying more and more commodities, to receive the highest possible rewards for our labours in order to meet our expenses, our loans and debts to which we have committed ourselves. And "when we see", as Jeremy Seabrook has put it, "how far a new generation is bonded to perpetual growth of the economy, we know things cannot possibly not go on like this. They have to. Our income depends on it. We must find refuge in the contradiction of a world where livelihood is at war with life ...

"But we know this is only buying time – that last commodity in the universal market. When George Bush the Younger refused to sign the Kyoto Convention on global warming on the grounds that nothing must be allowed to interfere with US economic interests, he was echoing the wisdom of George Bush the Elder, who spoke his famous words before the Rio summit that 'the American way of life is not up for negotiation'." [1]

Mankind makes its own reality but does not know it does so and how, and then faces the reality it has created as the inevitable conditions of life to which it has to adjust. The reality we have created is the acquisitive culture with its greed for possessions and wealth, and we then compete with or conquer those who stand in our way. The latter leads inevitably – given the cosmic powers of destruction of modern technological weaponry – to a global holocaust, and the former to the destruction of the ecosphere and the life-supporting system of our planet.

If we cannot find new directions, we have failed the life-promoting instincts of biological evolution. But we might remember Julian Huxley's statement that it is the mind which has become the agent of evolution. In other words we must learn to change our values and purposes. But how can we learn to think of a different and new future, how can children and adolescents acquire new ideas to transcend the present impasse?

In previous chapters I spoke of the satisfaction of work in workers' communities and the shared sense of responsibility for what they produce, of fresh approaches to education and the creation of a humanistic architecture. But behind work, school education and architecture there is the period responsible for a person's character development, the cradle of a civilisation's character, namely the home environment during infancy and childhood. But even here social conditions and cultural values play an important part.

The Reproduction of the Acquisitive Culture in the Parental Home.

Middle class parents who uphold freedom of enterprise in capitalist democracy will consider it their duty to transmit its values and its advantages to their children. For after all, they think it stands for the greatest happiness of the greatest number of people, and the opportunities it provides for acquiring wealth and prosperity assures our wellbeing, prestige and happiness. It is therefore the duty of parents to inculcate these ideals and practices in their children and to assure their success in a competitive world.

However, there is a problem: as the freedom to make as much money as possible is every person's right it must also apply to women and mothers. Women then are torn between two opposing urges: one, to have children and care for them and receive their love, the other, to make money and acquire their own possessions. Thus the mothers' emotional needs are divided, and if they give vent to the maternal instincts they have to divide their instincts of motherhood with the call of making money; their emotions are split and they find it difficult to devote themselves fully to the demands of their offspring and fulfil their natural instinct. Children are aware of their mother's discontent and confusion, and become anxious, apprehensive and tense like her. They want mother to be happy and receive love from her husband, so that she can give it to the child.

But all too often modern women feel the burden of being a mother in the frantic pursuit of money and participating in the men's world with its struggle for success, and project their resentments and insecurities upon their husband and children. There is no time to luxuriate in the pleasures of being together, to be cared for and experience their devotion to each other.

The race for material possessions, houses, cars, best furniture, best holidays, meeting the best people in the best restaurants and being seen as belonging to an élite, is meant to compensate for the love for which there is no time. Mothers and fathers will attempt to show that they love their children by showering them with ready-made tokens of love which can be bought in super-markets or in the best shops according to the latest fashion. And the child will learn to love the pre-packaged gift-offerings of affection, and they will want to acquire more and more, but still feel unsatisfied as they do not receive the love they want through intimate eye-to-eye, body-to-body contact. There is an endless amount of such ready-made, mass-produced symbols available, advertised and propagated in all the media: toys, play-things, happy little dollies, the latest in fashions and clothes and computer games, and the child will want to have them to fill the inner void and ease its tensions of loneliness, anxiety and frus-tration. But despite the multitude of such love substitutes there is the constant 'problem of having children', seeking advice from doctors, psychiatrists and experts, clever newspaper articles and books to teach parents how to 'cope with children'. But this leaves the problem unresolved, and many children become prob-lems, not only to themselves but to their parents and teachers.[2]

This then becomes the foundation for the psychological char-acteristics which 'modern man' inherits from his childhood, pre-paring him to become a member of the acquisitive society and uphold its values.

Referring to what Chris Woodhead and others have called the 'knowledge economy', Ivo Mosley writes: "Never before in human history has so much cleverness been used to such stupid ends ... In the face of an uncertain and alarming future, which holds little inspiration for present living, people fight off gloom and stupefaction by withdrawing into trivia, sensation-seeking or addictions to money, drugs, or power ... Dumbing down [is] ob-servable in almost all walks of life; politics, culture, civic ad-ministration, the media, science, education, even the law. It is so widespread that a new term has been coined: dumbocracy." [3]

Just at a time when we ought to exercise our intellectual and moral capacities to their fullest extent we have retreated to child-ish forms of self-expression, mocking the illusions of reason, as there seems to be no future to grow up for.

Plutocracy, Democracy and Social Capital.

There is no doubt that in the capitalist world of the West money rules and the pursuit of profit is the driving force for the creation of wealth. It is assumed that the wealth of a nation enhances its powers, benefits its citizens and improves their quality of life. The capitalist ruling class which owns a large part of the nation's wealth and controls its economy represents the modern plutocracy. Our plutocratic oligarchy has hijacked the ideals of democracy. The freedom of the individual is interpreted as freedom of enterprise, and the nation depends upon its entrepreneurs' successes or failures.

While oligarchy is generally described as a state governed by a small body of men who have the supreme power of the state in their hands, now their power derives from their wealth. We have an oligarchy of plutocrats made up of industrialists, bankers, financiers, while politicians collaborate with the money-owning class to support the economy.

But why is this called 'democratic'? Democracy is the rule of the people by the people who choose the government to represent their interests and their aspirations.

The ownership of wealth by a privileged class of entrepreneurs and capitalists, and a society controlled and governed by them cannot be considered a democracy. It is true that modern democracies uphold the freedom of speech and the expression of opinion, people's freedom to vote for political parties of their choice (often called elective dictatorship), but gives them little opportunity to share in the wealth of their society in any degree of equality, as long as the nation's wealth is held by a small minority who are determined to keep it and use the term democracy to justify their power. But if we are to take the word democracy for what it really means, then we would call the wealth of a country social wealth – the people's wealth.

Social wealth consists not just of the amount of money in circulation, a major part of which is owned by a privileged minority of plutocrats with the freedom to use it in which ever way they consider it advantageous to themselves. It must be remembered that the capital owned by the plutocrats derives from the labours of people who produce the commodities required to satisfy people's needs and provide medical care, food, clothing, and a million other products as well as music, theatre, the arts and literature, to stimulate and enlarge their mental horizons. Even these are promoted by speculators intent on making profit from their investment: their productions have to appeal to the widest possible public and meet its lowest common denominator in taste to ensure the highest possible profit. This even applies to many aspects of scientific research.

There is no doubt that there are people who are very good at making money. I have earlier mentioned some of the major influences in their lives which determined them to acquire and possess things, to become rich, not only to enjoy the luxuries they can buy but also to be known and admired and enjoy their powers in society. They are driven by a compulsion to make money, but even when they have become very rich and can buy whatever they want, their compulsions do not cease and they want more and more money and more and more luxuries.

It must be admitted that there is a fascination with gambling at the stock exchange, financial speculation and many other ways of making money in the casino of capitalism, but one would expect 'normal people' to leave the casino as soon as they had made as much money as they needed to buy themselves the things they had always wanted. The obsessive gamblers, on the other hand, continue to risk their winnings in the casino in their determination to make more.

However, the people who are obsessed with money and profit-making, and have the talent to succeed, can be very useful.

This brings us back to the creation of work communities which need the support of some capital to get them started. This would require the help of government-sponsored banks specifically committed to this purpose. They could be called workers' enterprise banks and would not charge interest, or would keep it very low. A social-democratic government sympathetic to the creation of such communities would provide not only the necessary money to start them but also provide access to economists to determine

119

the market potentials for their produce. They would contribute to the wealth of the nation, serve the people and would not be driven solely by the profit motive, even though they would expect to receive a fair share of their income.

The work communities I have described are in the first instance meant for workshops and small to medium size factories. They would be models for a democratic and humanistic mode of production.

But this is only a beginning. Modern societies need large-scale industries to serve the needs of the nation, and beyond that of a wider community of nations to provide clean water, electricity, oil, petrol, and chemicals used in producing modern materials such as plastics and chemical fibres; we need the pharmacological industry which provides medicine with a vast array of drugs; sanitation; motor cars, aeroplanes and public transport; the electronic industry for communication in radio, television and computers. These are just some of the large-scale industries essential for what we call civilised living.

The question then arises: Where does the capital come from to finance them? It is all very well to accuse the capitalist system for its adverse influence upon society, but one must recognise that it has created a vast range of industries which have improved the quality of life in many respects and provided facilities which were undreamt of only a century ago. The capitalist of the modern era may have acquired the initial capital for his enterprises through his personal wealth which he has inherited, or from wealthy friends and relatives, from banks and particularly from the stock market. He is a person with a talent for persuading people of the viability and profitability of his project; he would have a talent for self-promotion to attract investors. Above all he would have a sound instinct for technological innovations which could be utilised in the production of new commodities which meet the demands of the public and he would be ready to take risks in keeping with his gambling instincts.

Investment banks and financial corporations know how to kindle a speculative mania which is an inevitable feature of the market system at times of a conjunction between a growing middle class and technological innovations. Of course many things can go wrong, as we have seen in the Twenties and Thirties. And we have seen it again when the high-tech bubble burst and caused the largest recession in the stock market since the Thirties, making large corporations bankrupt and depriving many people of their investments and pensions.

Insofar as energy supplies are an essential part of the nations's economy they ought to be included in our project for democratic modes of production, but they are owned and administered by huge private corporations who would not be prepared to relinquish their powers. Oil companies like Exxon, Shell, and BP dominate the exploitation and refinement of oil and petrol, and have established international trade organisations which would be difficult to disrupt. In any case their capital value is so enormous (it has been said that their wealth is greater than that of the whole of the United States), and their influence upon the economy and international trade would make it almost impossible for any particular nation to acquire ownership and control over them. It would therefore be best to leave them as they are. But this would not preclude governments from keeping an eye on them to prevent the oil producers from harming the national economy by raising their prices and dictating the politics of nations in order to serve the interests of their global cartels.

It is also the responsibility of a social-democratic government to care for its citizens who are mentally or physically disabled and unable to work, and to support them.

But where is the money to come from to pay for the generous intention of real democracy devoted to the care of its citizens?

It is necessary to discriminate between non-returnable public expenditure and returnable expenditure. This is particularly obvious in public transport where the government investment in a good and efficient transport system will be repaid by the travelling public through the fares they pay for their journeys. It has always been puzzling to me that ministers of transport and chancellors of the exchequer consider the capital invested as non-returnable and money lost to the Treasury, whereas private companies pay to acquire the ownership of railways and make large investments to make a profit. Where do they think the profit will come from? The answer is from the fare-paying public, of course. So they put the fares up and save money by reducing expenditure on rail maintenance and the provision of new and better trains. This to me and to every passenger and the general public appears to be quite mad. Therefore, it seems common sense that if the government invests in railways and underground systems to satisfy and attract passengers, as well as in goods trains, the cost of their investment would be repaid by the passengers and freight companies which use the railways.

In fact, building a good railway system improves the revenues for the Chancellor of the Exchequer and the Ministry of Transport; what it requires is good design, intelligent planning and a devoted workforce. It would also and above all have the beneficial effect of reducing the misery of traffic congestion on the motorways and the roads in towns and in the countryside. The proselytisers of monetarism and budgetary prudence have made motorway journeys a nightmare, a very frustrating and stressful experience, with outbursts of bad temper and road rage. A well-designed transport system would also reduce carbon dioxide emission and air pollution.

A satisfactory National Health Service – although a non-returnable expenditure as it would not receive revenues from its patients (even while it may be reasonable for those who can afford it to make a contribution), would nevertheless save large amounts of money insofar as patients who are returned to health would be able to work again instead of having to wait for months and even years to see a consultant before they can receive appropriate treatment and the operations they require. But if their treatment is delayed for a long time and patients are left in pain and unable to work, the Chancellor of the Exchequer and the Inland Revenue lose a lot of money due to loss of production and income tax contributions.

It is amazing that nobody seems to recognise this obvious fact. Governments and councils do not seem to take into account the revenue they can receive from investment in a good public transport and public health system, and the rents from decent housing. We are dealing here with a form of monetary fetishism which sees capital as an abstract and fixed entity which accountants can measure and control in their calculations of available capital and acceptable expenditure, in order to keep within the budget which puts a limit to the money available for public spending. This obsession with fixed capital, which has to be retained and preserved, and their calculations of how much capital can be spent reduces the government's investment in the social services. This is an upside-down way of dealing with the needs and quality of life of its citizens.

Trusting the Workers.

A sane administration would first of all examine what improvements have to be made to serve the country's well-being, and then consider how the money can be found. Instead of being tied to the accountant's assessment of sums available at a given moment, it needs some long-term thinking towards 'accrual-based accounting', which, according to Neil Kinnock, the European Commission expects to adopt in the future. This would also mean that managers and administrators trust the staff they employ and have confidence in their ability to perform their task: for the chief capital available to the nation is its workers. It is they who produce wealth and by their work provide for the people's needs and aspirations. If the government and their appointees, and indeed any employer, want to bring the best out in people, to liberate their productive and intellectual potentials, it has to treat them with respect, and acknowledge their skills and their judgement and encourage their initiative, so that the people who work for them can feel a measure of pride and self-respect in their work: they need to feel appreciated so that they can appreciate the organisation they work for.

The Times, Tuesday 3 September 2002, reports that "the public sector faces an 'imminent staff crisis' because young people no longer want to work in it." The Audit Commission's report states that "the public sector's age-profile represents a 'demographic time-bomb', because once older workers retired no one would fill their places." The Audit Commission found that the single biggest thing that turns nurses, doctors, teachers and policemen off is paperwork and too much bureaucracy. They feel stressed and they don't have enough autonomy. Upon asking former public service professionals why they had left, they answered that it was the stress caused by too much bureaucracy and paperwork, which easily topped the list cited by nearly 18% of those interviewed. Talk to anyone working in the health service, schools or the police and it is immediately obvious what a demoralising, all-pervasive problem this has become.

"Staff across all public services are leaving in droves because they are overwhelmed by government targets, paperwork, lack of resources and long working hours ... Most are leaving because of 'negative experiences' rather than being attracted by higher pay in the private sector.

"Andrew Foster, the Audit Commission controller, warned the Government that its pledge to recruit thousands of extra nurses and doctors would never be fulfilled unless the image of the public sector changed and both the government and local employers value their staff more ...

"The commission called on the Government and employers to collect much better data on the reasons why staff resigned." [4]

Yes, indeed. But if employers of public enterprises want their staff to be productive and efficient and show some enthusiasm for what they are doing, they have to receive recognition and appreciation. In the health services doctors and nurses are paid strictly controlled, minimum wages according to the budget assigned to them; junior doctors in hospitals frequently have to work seventy or eighty hours a week, leaving them exhausted and harassed and resentful at not be able to do their work as they feel they should.

As a secretary working in a major London hospital has informed me in a private communication:

Under the name of clinical governance the National Health Service is subjected to a remorseless scrutiny and rules which are contradictory and highly confusing. Clinical governance requires that everything is documented, every patient-doctor interaction, the decisions a doctor makes, has to be written down in an endless task of form-filling, to prevent patients from suing the NHS for neglect. Copies of diagnoses and of prescriptions must be kept in the patient's notes and sent to their GP. But, to be honest, no one has time to properly read the avalanche of papers and forms generated by the system, but it has to be done for the record, in case of complaints. And the doctors are subject to accountability. However, most clinicians do not trust the new system and often manage to record only what in their expert view is clinically necessary. But while they manage to avoid the worst pitfalls of 'transparency', they are still subject to 'accountability'. The process involves each clinician attending a series of meetings to discuss his or her 'job plan', which has to be appraised and then audited by outside bodies. The 'appraisals' are conducted by other clinicians and a senior bureaucrat. The bureaucrat knows nothing about clinical practice, and the other consultant usually works in a different discipline from the clinician under review. How can he and the bureaucrat know if the best clinical practice is being followed? They can't.

My correspondent continues:

Whatever the stated aims of clinical governance are, its effect is to undermine existing good practice. Nurses do not have time to fill in all the forms and look after patients, but if they have to fill in the forms the patient care suffers. Junior doctors are stressed by the continual scrutiny, the form filling and meetings and are intimidated by the appraisals and exhausted by the extraordinary long hours they have to work, often seventy, up to eighty hours a week. Senior doctors are deeply resentful and they are right to be so. After years of dedicated service they are being told very clearly that they must justify their presence in the NHS, but as experienced professionals they also know that added levels of bureaucracy can only be disastrous. But if doctors are not trusted and do not show confidence in their work, the patient will not feel confident that he is getting the best possible treatment. Trust has always been an important factor in the successful treatment of patients who want to trust their doctor and feel that he is taking a personal interest in them. Doctors have always known this, the bureaucracy apparently does not.

My informant also happens to be a writer and poet, and expresses her feelings about the situation in the National Health Service in the following manner:

> While I have a desire to do some small good in society, my masters feel that I am doing good by summoning perfectly innocent clinicians to interminable meetings, photocopying forests of paper, typing letters of admonition, endless drafts of reports, protocols and guidelines, and helping them – my masters – inflict such stress on the doctors and nurses who are trying to give help to the suffering masses and can't because they can't move for paper and can't think straight for the sheer quantity of rules and regulations they have to remember and act in accordance with, to say nothing of all the forms – goodness, the forms – which they are required by law to complete. And everybody seems to think its normal, rational – blimey!

There are now, February 2003, as many managers and administrators in the NHS as doctors and nurses, and there are more controls and regulations imposed by the government in Britain then there were in Soviet Russia. But the more rules are imposed upon the workers, the more resentful and incompetent they become: "If the authorities don't respect or trust us, then we won't respect them. If they don't trust our work, then we won't trust their rules." A kind of unconscious class war takes place as we have seen in the abysmal incompetence of industry in the Soviet Union.

But the same thing could be said about the situation in the teaching profession. No wonder young people do not want to become teachers, and the older ones are leaving as soon as they can.

At the bottom of all this unbelievable mismanagement is the

government's professed need to keep within the limits of the budget and the capital available to be spent on medical care, education, transport, the reduction of crime and other social services.

Where then is the money to come from to finance, kick-start, a real democracy? We have to find out now how a truly democratic society can get the money necessary to increase the wealth of the people and improve the social services.

What to do with the Capitalists.

What I would call a radical humanism not only pronounces the ideals of a just society but is resolved to put them into practice. The money successful capitalists make goes into their own pockets and as far as the casino of capitalism is concerned represents a loss to its resources, and if the losses involved are too large they could endanger its solvency. A wise casino therefore would put a ceiling to the size of its punters' bets and to their winnings (some casinos actually have rules to this effect).

The same applies to the budget and financial affairs of a nation. The vast profits made by its capitalist gamblers, entrepreneurs and financial speculators represent a loss to the Treasury and to the nation's corporate wealth. But the gamblers do not think about the casino's problems, nor do they feel responsible for it or for the problems of their society. They will find new profitable uses for their winnings by taking over other companies or investing in new projects which they think can be made profitable. They will appeal to people's fantasies about the new possessions available and the excitements they offer.

Finance companies and banks flood people's homes with advertisements offering cheap, competitive and easy loans to acquire the possessions they crave for, and a vast array of luxury goods are advertised in the newspapers and journals and on television to arouse their desires for ever new acquisitions as compensation for their boredom and insecurity. Our capitalist gamblers offer all kinds of commodities and mortgages for acquiring houses and flats, expensive treatment for beauty and perfect health to inflame the consumerist mania. The point is that while they stimulate the public's hunger for commodities and services which promise instant happiness – which more often than not turn out to be disappointing and useless – they waste the country's economic resources which could be spent on what is useful and necessary.

This is borne out in a recent investigation by Brunel University, which finds that the desire among women to improve their mood created a new addiction – shopping bulimia. Shopping bulimics indulge in retail therapy, but feel guilty when they get home and take the items back. More than half of the women questioned confess to indulging in shopping bulimia, which is growing fast among women, by going shopping and then feel disappointed and guilty. This is where we see parallels with disorders such as bulimia. Tamira King of Brunel University found that tell-tale signs include keeping receipts, clothes with labels still attached, and hiding shopping bags.

The gold of human creativity and productive skills is turned into rubbish. The urge to show one's abilities, to make things and to communicate one's thoughts is turned into junk: junk mail, junk products and junk culture. The claims made by the capitalist fraternity that the wealth they acquire will percolate down to the people and improve their lives, have been shown to be false. They not only try their best to persuade people to buy disappointing and useless commodities and to spend a large part of their income and their savings on them, but actually misuse the country's productive capacities and diminish its wealth. They impoverish the nation both spiritually as well as economically.

I therefore propose that a democratic society should impose a limit to the winnings of its (capitalist) gamblers. It should not exclude them, i.e. expropriate them, but use their talents for making large fortunes for the benefit of the people. To this end the capital which they have amassed and consider their own private property should not exceed eight million pounds, at its present value at the time I am writing in 2003, and everything beyond that should be returned to the nation. Their annual income from this sum if invested in a saving account or bonds would provide them with a return of roughly £320,000 annually, or about £6,000 per week. If we take the average earnings, including the skilled workers and the middle classes, as £35,000 per year, or £650 per week, it represents only a tenth of the amount which the capitalist entrepreneurs would receive. Thus the successful entrepreneur with a fortune of £8,000,000 is left with more than ten times the income of the average population.

Perhaps another, more simple, way of ploughing a great part of the wealth of the super rich back into society to be converted into social wealth would be to charge a very high rate of tax, about 95%, on an income of over £350,000 per year, perhaps called supertax. The specific details of such arrangements and legislation could be fruitfully discussed by economists and financial experts who are sympathetic to the ideas of a social democracy. I think that a capital of £8,000,000 or an income of £350,000 a year could be a satisfactory incentive for the players in the capitalist casino to exercise their entrepreneurial abilities.

Just as I am writing this, 20th June 2003, Peter Hain, the left-wing leader of the House of Commons has announced his plan to tax the rich more to ensure that hardworking middle income families and the lower paid get a better deal by making those at the top of the pay-scale contribute more through higher taxes. By maintaining the 22% basic rate of taxation the current income level of £35,000–£50,000 could mean that such middle class earners would be better off. However, he plans to raise taxes for those earning from £75,000–£100,000 by 50%, which would affect the majority of the successful and socially useful entrepreneurs, and may disincentivise them. I would propose keeping their tax level to 40% as before. Peter Hain falls into the trap of being accused of taxing the rich in order to help those of the lower and middle income bracket, and shows a confusion about what we mean by 'rich'. What we have to do is encourage the socially useful entrepreneur, but regain the wealth of the super rich – those who earn more than £350,000 per year or £6,000 per week – for society

As could be expected, Anthony Hilton, the Financial Editor of the *Evening Standard*, came up with a riposte to Peter Hain:

"The big economic discovery of the Eighties was the Laffer

curve, which, like most economic theory, was common sense dressed up as science. Its basic proposition was that if governments take off in tax most of what people earn, then they won't work very hard. If, however, government cuts tax as far as it reasonably can, people will have the motivation to work harder, and that will generate significant extra wealth which in turn will yield tax. A virtuous circle is created whereby the extra growth is more than enough to make good the revenue lost by the initial tax cuts. Ronald Reagan was converted to this idea in the 1980s. Since then it has swept the world, and with good reason. It has been demonstrated time and again that low-tax economies are more flexible, more dynamic and more innovative than high-tax ones ... Then, it was estimated you have to tax the rich at 90% to knock a couple of pennies off income tax for the rest of the country." [5]

In fact Peter Hain is not radical enough; it shows the futility of tinkering with the established system and its conceptual paradigm, namely the virtue of free enterprise.

Also the future of the Stock Exchange will have to be investigated. There would have to be strict rules to prevent the flight of capital abroad. I guess that not many of our ultra-rich entrepreneurs would want to emigrate to try their luck in foreign countries.

If we consider that there are many executives, directors and owners of large enterprises who receive £10,000,000 per year in wages and bonuses, often topped up by a £10,000,000 windfall, we might ask what they do with it. Perhaps they will buy themselves more luxury houses, large yachts, or private aeroplanes, even while the airspace is already dangerously overcrowded, or spend millions on entertaining other rich and famous individuals, in order to claim them as their friends. These are only just a few examples of useless money spent by the billionaire financial wizards and take-over freaks who gamble in order to make more and more money and keep their name among the élite of capitalism.

The problem is that in a society which is indoctrinated by the

virtues of the profit motive and consumerism, they have become
the role models particularly for the young who feel that they have
to imitate them. Nothing is enough, 'I want it all, become rich
by any way possible', in a frantic pursuit of a collective mania,
which is regarded as the purpose of life. The chase to belong to
'the successful', the famous and the rich, is never quite satisfied
and loses all sense of reality. The quest for recognition becomes
relentless, and greed devours everything that the system can offer, including nature's resources. Those who are not affected by
this disease remain relatively poor in comparison and are not regarded as successful members of society. Thus the liberal creed
of the greatest happiness for the greatest number of people made
possible by the freedom of enterprise has turned out in practice
as a programme for the greatest possible acquisition of wealth
for the capitalist plutocrats, which a restless public strives to
imitate, and being unable to do so is left with a sense of failure.

What about Unemployment? How can we avert it?

When a lot of work needs to be done to improve the standard of
life for the 'ordinary' people, when many are deprived of basic
needs, there is a section of the population who are not allowed
to work by the chronic malaise of unemployment which is characteristic of capitalistic societies even in our time. Germany,
which for long has been called the powerhouse of the European
economy, has over 4 million people out of work, and most major countries in Europe have over 2 million, with the exception
of England which for the time being has managed to keep it down
to about 1. 3 million.

This paradox which amounts to a malaise in the body of capitalist society is due to the dominance of major corporations which
follow their own interests concerned with the profitability of their
product and frequently fail to foresee correctly the size of demand among the consumers. In their optimistic assessment of the
potential market for their products they over-invest and over-
produce to find that their predictions have been unrealistic and
have to lay-off large parts of their workers, in order to reduce

costs and to avoid bankruptcy, and close many of their factories. This not only affects actual producers but also the financial organisations who had invested in them and also offer their financial 'products' to the public which in times of recession cannot afford to buy them. This is an old story which in recent times has led to the loss of billions of pounds and the bankruptcy of many leading industrial and financial organisations committed to boosting the expectations of the electronic, high-tech areas of industry.

It is happening again. In the words of Warren Buffett, the second richest man in the world, "the world economy is paying the price for the dot com hype". In an interview he said that the debts incurred in the periods when markets disconnect from the real world and unscrupulous U.S. executives took advantage of the late 1990 stock market hype, you had "an erosion of the accountant's standing, and to some extent in executive behaviour." He refers to the collapse of some of the major corporations who put their hope into the fast-growing demands for electronic, high-tech, computer-led industries and were able to convince financial organisations and shareholders to invest huge amounts of money in the new product which was to revolutionise industry. In England we have seen the collapse of Marconi, the offshoot of GEC, England's major engineering company whose capital was squandered in the rush of excitement about the profits to be made in the new computerised world in which everybody wanted to participate. The expectations of huge fortunes to be made lost touch with reality. Their shares fell from £12 to 1.5p.

The collapse of major financial and industrial corporations not only affected millions of shareholders but has led to a global recession. It has also led to a profound mistrust of the leading finance houses and investment banks, the stockbrokers and investment analysts whose corrupt practices are well-documented, undermining the public's respect and admiration for the powerful engines of capitalism. This has not only led to an economic recession but also to a psychological depression among the gamblers in the casino of capitalism as well as the public at large.

It is not only the chronic unemployment of industrial workers which in the past, as for instance in the Great Depression of the early Thirties, led to an economic breakdown and catastrophic social upheavals but now also affects office workers, who work long hours sitting in front of their monitors exhausted and stressed about the insecurity of their job, as well as industrial and financial managers haunted by a sense of responsibility for the possible failure of their company.

Banks and financial corporations compete with each other in their attempt to provide the most attractive loans for people to acquire all kinds of goods which they have never heard of, but are now made to appear absolute necessities, and get people back to play their role as consumers in order to stimulate the economy. It creates restlessness and confusion as well as a nagging sense of dissatisfaction in the mind of the consumers, feeling that they must acquire the goods which are offered, or rather, pressed upon them, even while they are not really sure that they want them but must have, and if it involves them with a burden of debts which they are not sure how to repay.

But what is it all for? To keep business going by selling a mass of useless products and stimulating the public's greed and craving for attention as well as young people's fantasies of joining the ranks of the celebrities. One may compare this to a madhouse whose patients often rush around and do things which mean nothing – a manic-depressive, anxiety-ridden world which psychiatrists are trying to understand, without much hope.

This brings me back to the role workers' communities can play in creating a measure of sanity in social life. They would not be subject to the iron laws of capitalism, which depend upon the profit motive and the culture of consumerism to ensure the widest possible market for their produce by whatever means their sales experts can dream up, without much consideration or care for people's actual needs. A workers' community would in the first place be in direct person-to-person contact with its customers, and could assess what people want to buy and organise their production accordingly. They would provide a social service. When they expand into small factories on the outskirts of towns, they would still be within contact with their own locality and with their potential customers. Above all they would maintain a state of mind and a sense of purpose committed to the needs of the public.

I have suggested earlier that the findings of social scientists about what people need and what they consider important should be made available to the producers. I should here like to hazard a guess that people would want:

(1) to live in decent homes with easy access to open spaces.

(2) the availability of good and healthy food.

(3) good medical treatment for everybody who needs it, without discrimination between those who are rich enough to afford private medicine and the average citizen who can't afford it.

(4) a good education for everybody, which would develop young people's talents and not only prepare them for earning a decent living but also ensure their self-respect as worthy contributors to the nation's material and spiritual well-being.

(5) that decisive efforts should be made to reduce the level of crime and violence particularly among the young, which has made life in inner cities and even in country areas insecure and frightening in many cases.

(6) the provision of a decent transport system which makes people's journeys more comfortable and less stressful.

(7) job security, in order to eliminate the anxiety of becoming unemployed.

These demands which express basic needs as well the hopes of most people are both practical as well as realistic. They need the close co-operation between the producers and the people's elected representatives in government and its legislators.

We shall have to examine the economics of communal production, demand and supply; the price of commodities, distribution and sales; profit sharing and the worker's income.

There are other concerns which affect people and cause anxiety but are more problematic and they need a re-examination of our ways of thinking and judgements. While people want to have decent homes they also want to have a satisfying and happy home life, free from the stresses and anxieties experienced by many families, where fathers and mothers are too busy going out to work in order to earn a lucrative income while there is not enough time for their children and the enjoyment of caring for them. In this country more than a quarter of families are one parent families and this is widely recognised as a source of deprivation, for children need a mother and a father's loving attention to develop a balanced personality. The explosion of criminal and aggressive behaviour among young people is beginning to be understood as being due to an absence of the paternal role model and a happy relationship between fathers and mothers, necessary for a person's sense of direction and purpose.

We are mass-producing a generation without a future. The widespread conscious or preconscious anxiety about the destruction of the biosphere, the life-supporting system of this planet, and hundreds of millions not getting enough food to survive fills many people with pessimism about the meaning and purpose of life; we no longer believe our own beliefs. We are all too aware of the pollution of the atmosphere, the seas and the rivers, and the disappearance, the dying out of once familiar animal species, and we realise now that these manifestations of the man-made damage to nature, the harm to the animal world is not confined to our own natural environment but afflicts the whole globe.

CHAPTER 9

Towards Global Sanity

The Ecological Catastrophe.

Modern technology has opened up the planet and penetrated the old boundaries between nations, cultures and races. But it is not a planet free from the ancient, paranoid obsessions with tribal, religious and racial enmities. With the unprecedented freedom of travel and information the planet has become smaller, we have become aware of parts of the world which previously were far away, knew little about and did not affect our traditions and beliefs. We were enshrined in our own problems and not concerned with countries and cultures which were outside our own sphere of interest. But now September 11th 2001 has forced us to recognise that religious fanatics and terrorists are a threat to our own civilisation. What was considered a completely alien culture had erupted into the Western world. Suddenly the shameful barbarism of the Dark Ages, which we thought we had overcome long ago, invaded the present and has become real.

Another aspect of the open planet is our awareness of the poverty of large parts of mankind; hundreds of millions are starving, and many more are undernourished and denied access to clean water and sanitation. We are becoming conscious of mankind's responsibility for the fate of our planet, as modern science and technology have penetrated the old barriers and turned all humans into a community from which we cannot escape. We have become responsible for the earth and the biosphere, and our actions, wherever we are and to whatever culture we belong, affect the life, for good or for evil, of all of us. We face the destruction of the primeval forests by large-scale and irresponsible deforestation which has depleted the oxygen in the air we breathe, the pollution of the seas and rivers, the vastly increased emission of

136

carbon monoxide into the atmosphere. We face large-scale soil erosion due to industrial forms of agriculture, which are subsidised by more than three hundred billion dollars each year.

The pollution of the sea and rivers by chemical discharge and industrial waste from nuclear processing plants and oil spills from ships has led to the despoilation of marine life and the death of 50% of all fishes, while 25% of the waters in the seas and rivers are over-fished.

Chemical pollution of the natural environment and of arable land has caused a wide range of diseases and the extermination of many animal species. Chemical and CO_2 pollution of the atmosphere has produced the greenhouse effect and global warming which is responsible for dramatic climate changes. "The UN Intergovernmental Panel of Climate Change warns that temperatures could rise by a global average of 5.8°C ... and create weather-related disasters such as droughts or floods in large areas of the globe; they have already increased by 160% between 1975 and 2001, killing 440,000 people and causing $480 billion worth of damage in the 1990s alone."[1]

It is anticipated that in the next four decades many areas of low-lying land will be flooded and submerged by the rising levels of the oceans.

At international conferences and world summits as well as international environmental treaties to avoid ecological catastrophes, the advanced countries of the world proclaim their intention to rescue the underdeveloped nations from their poverty and hunger by providing them with modern industrial forms of production.

This is to be achieved in the following ways:

1) through loans from financial corporations and investment banks.

2) by establishing Western style industries run by multinational corporations.

3) by raising agricultural productivity through chemical fertilisers supplied by the major chemical corporations.

4) by modern machinery for the establishment of efficient mass-production methods in local factories.

5) by making pharmaceutical products available for the treat-

ment of diseases among the population and improving the health of their cattle, thereby increasing meat and milk production to provide sufficient nourishment for the indigenous populations.

The financial and industrial establishments of the West are prepared to spend huge amounts of money in the effort to improve the standard of living among the impoverished people of the underdeveloped world and to restore the global environment. And everybody now agrees that this is a task of vital importance for all of us. The major corporations who are ready to provide the expenditure required would consider it self-evident that they would receive a return for their investment and avoid making huge losses which would threaten them with bankruptcy.

But we must take into account that behind what appear to be perfectly laudable and responsible considerations there is the profit motive which is fundamental to capitalist thinking. In order to ensure that their enterprises are profitable they have to acquire raw materials at the cheapest possible price for the production of commodities to sell in the West. They are also on the lookout for cheap labour in order to reduce the cost of production and expenditure in order to sell their products in Western countries at a competitive price.

The new world market which has opened up for them meets those requirements and provides an ideal opportunity for capitalist enterprises. But their calculations have been too simplistic and over-optimistic. They anticipated ready access to cheap raw materials and a huge market for their products, but the reality which they have created by their endeavours has turned out to be different, and the dreams of the wonders of modern technology able to provide a world of plenty have turned into nightmares. They are pilloried at the world summits, condemned by experts and by an increasing part of public opinion.

The industrial conglomerates saw the vast areas of the underdeveloped world opening up to them as raw materials to be used for their purposes: the forests of the world for logging and convertion into timber for various construction projects; the ground as an apparently inexhaustible treasure to be mined for copper, iron and nickel, and drilled for oil and gas. The chemical industries saw a huge market as more chemicals were needed for virtually every manufactured product – from motor cars to synthetic materials for clothes, home and office appliances and computer-manufacturing industries, and for the universal use of plastics in machines, textiles, paper and packaging. The industrialisation of agriculture and the force-feeding of the land with chemical fertilisers in order to obtain the largest possible quantity of specialised products drove peasants from their land and forced them to work in urban areas in order to support themselves, turning them into a new proletariat, the unskilled labourers living in poverty and squalor.

Western style industrialisation and in particular the system of industrial agriculture has 'enclosed' farmland, forcing peasants off their land, so that it can be used for high-priced export products instead of the traditional diverse crops for the local population. Land enclosure has forced untold millions of peasants across the world to lose their land, their community and traditions. The tragedy is that the land controlled and owned by the multinational corporations deprives the local population of staple foods to feed their families and their communities. Global corporations force local peasants to produce high profit luxury foods while local populations are deprived of essentials. In Africa, for example, where severe famines have occurred during the last decade, industrial agriculture achieved record yields for its cash crops, while the local population went hungry.

One can classify the world's population into three groups: there are about 1.2 billion people who consume the equivalent of 850 kg each year, mostly in the form of animal products and mixed foods; there are another 3.5 billion people whose food intake sustains them, consuming the equivalent of 350 kg of grain in a mixed diet; and there are 1.3 billion who survive on 150 kg, leaving them undernourished and hungry, and many starve.

The methods adopted by most Western governments and the major corporations to reduce world hunger and avert ecological disasters are focussed on producing ever higher yields of specific products for export, and are actually increasing world hunger and causing environmental and social disasters. They not only dramatically increase the impoverishment of billions of people to an extent we have never seen before, even during the worst periods

139

of the Industrial Revolution, but world-wide pollution of the air, the rivers and the seas, the greenhouse effect, and damage to the ozone layer which made the emergence of life on this planet possible in the first place.

We have to revolutionise our approach to feeding the world. The focus has to be on supporting and encouraging local agriculture where people can live close to or on the land, grow food for their own communities and use ecologically sustainable techniques. It can be reasonably objected that this type of village agriculture employing the traditional skills to serve local communities cannot possibly be applied to the 'advanced' countries and their multi-million towns and modes of scientific, technological mass production; nor can their money-centred economy be abolished, as we cannot expect to turn back the clock of history to a time where mankind stood before the Industrial Revolution.

However, the crisis which has befallen the Western world, which I have attempted to show in previous chapters, and the awareness of a global crisis in which we are all involved, makes it increasingly obvious that radical changes are necessary. While it would be unrealistic to attempt a return to a pre-industrial way of life in the Western world, it is quite realistic and necessary in the underdeveloped countries where industrialisation and mass production is imposed from the outside with often catastrophic results. For them it is essential to revert back to their traditional forms of production and agricultural practice to which they are accustomed. It would not only repair the spiritual alienation and emotional distress caused by the imposition of an alien culture but would rehabilitate their long-acquired skills. Indeed, they would regain the efficiency of agricultural production, enabling them to exercise their traditional craftsmanship in the production of the commodities they need. They have to be given back the land which was theirs before it was taken from them by foreign corporations who are determined to use it for their own purpose, namely to export products which they consider profitable in the Western markets while impoverishing their farmers.[2]

We in the West are probably not aware that people of the 'backward' countries have (or at least, until recently) a close contact with their natural environment: the land in which they live, the forests around them, the sea and the rivers, their traditional skills to make tools and to use them to plough and sow, to harvest, to cultivate the grassland to feed their cows and their cattle for milk and for meat, and build their homes. They did not have much machinery but the tools they made and used were owned by the community and those who worked with them. From the point of view of our own present civilisation, they did not have a high standard of living, but they were not poor in their own eyes. (If this seems like a romantic view of these peoples' way of life, we shall have to add the occurrence of natural disasters, such as droughts, floods, and storms, as well as the ancient obsessions with the rituals of tribal warfare.)

In ancient cultures the ideals of masculinity are associated with a man's ability to produce on the behalf of the community and to protect it, whereas in Western societies manhood is measured in terms of ownership of land or money, and in terms of power over others. The big man in industrial society is also the richest and most successful. He has the most of what society needs or wants.

In an earlier chapter I have suggested that social investigators should ask people what they think they need most. I think that the most important and fundamental needs of the 'backward' countries are:

1) to reclaim their land to avoid further disasters;
2) to produce adequate and nourishing food;
3) to have a sufficient supply of clean drinking water; and
4) to have adequate sanitation.

Enabling Third World Peasants to Help Themselves.

The indigenous people must be given their lands back to cultivate them in their traditional ways and rehabilitate the land from the damage it suffered from large-scale industrial agriculture and return to organic and diversified farming. The Rio Earth Summit (1992) proclaimed: "It is urgent to arrest land degradation and launch conservation and rehabilitation programmes in the most critically affected and vulnerable areas." High-tech farming methods which in the West have yielded a high degree of productivity have lead to a catastrophic decline of productivity in the underdeveloped world and indeed world-wide. "The world-wide loss of [agricultural production] due to soil erosion alone is estimated to be the equivalent of twenty million tons of grain per year." "Globally, each year, there continues to be a net loss of twenty-six billion tons of soil from erosion; human-induced [land erosion by chemical fertilisers] encroaches on six million hectares of once productive land; and up to 2.5 million hectares of prime agricultural lands are abandoned" by its native peasants. "In total, an estimated 552 million hectares [equivalent to 38% of agricultural land worldwide] have been degraded by unsustainable agricultural practices between 1945 and 1990" ... On the other hand, "support for organic, soil conserving forms of agriculture accounts for only 2% of the total agricultural budgets in industrial countries", while "worldwide, government subsidies for industrial forms of agriculture amount to more than $313 billion each year."

While intense, specialised farming methods erode the land, water shortages affect the lives of millions of people. "According to the UN, 41% of the world's population, some 2.3 billion people live in 'water-stressed' areas – where water shortages are frequent. In 2002, this killed over 7 million people, and 1.2 billion people worldwide drink polluted water, causing hundreds of millions of cases of water-related diseases every year; and 6000 children die every day through drinking polluted water."

"The general objective is to make certain that adequate supplies of water of good quality are maintained for the entire population of this planet" ... "All States could initiate ... programmes for the protection, conservation and rational use of [surface and groundwater] resources on a sustainable basis." (Rio, 1992) But as we can see they have lamentably failed to do so.[3]

The fourth of the necessary requirements basic for the rehabilitation of the underdeveloped countries is the provision of sanitation. Many of the small peasant farmers who were forced to leave their land as they were made 'surplus to requirement' by modern farming methods and had to move to urban areas to try making a living, found themselves in overcrowded and squalid shanty-towns, which lacked adequate sanitation and drainage systems, and subjected to rampant diseases which particularly affected the children.

Thus the basic needs for the improvement of life amongst something like 45% of the world's population are, to repeat: food, water, reclaiming their land and sanitation. While speaking of the problems of the Western world, I pointed to more humane forms of production by the establishment of "intelligent workers' communities", to the need of a humanistic architecture, to a system of education which stimulates its pupils and brings out the best in them according to their talents, and to the need to contain the powers of capitalism. In the third world education is provided by their community which teaches them their traditional customs and beliefs, while their skills are taught by the mothers and fathers and the grown-up males of the community. Their community feelings do not have to be encouraged for they are part of their traditional way of life.

The first and most fundamental step, therefore, is to return the land to its original owners and enable them to rebuild their lives in their ancient methods of small-scale, diverse organic farming. To make this possible would mean – to use Marx's words – to expropriate the expropriators. But this no longer implies a revolution of the working class against its capitalist exploiters as in the Western world; it is now a global problem, and does not mean to smash capitalism but to transform its policies in its relationship to the new global economy. This is mainly a responsibility of the advanced countries whose economies are dominated by the multi-national corporations which have expropriated the native farmers and imposed Western technology of mass production. It is not merely a problem which faces the underdeveloped areas but all of humanity, and we must acknowledge the fact that the advanced countries are largely responsible for it and should feel duty-bound to change their policies, which can be compared to a cancer which threatens to invade the whole organism of life on the planet.

We must learn not to think we know better than the so-called primitive people and impose our ideas upon them; we have to

143

listen to what help they need to start the process of self-rehabilitation. The UN should be committed to sending agriculturalists to consult the local population and to help local farmers to start the work of the rehabilitation and cultivation of their land. It is most likely that in the first instance they would need a supply of crop seed to start the season, tools and some machinery, which should be sent to them free of charge. The expenditure of providing teams of consultants as well as tools and machines should not be regarded as an investment but as an act of restitution for the damage Western industrial and financial corporations have inflicted upon their lands and upon the global ecology. The cost of this commitment would only be a fraction of the money spent on enforced industrialisation.

As one Indian farmer's wife put it succinctly: "If Britain wants to give money to help us it should come to the farmers directly. That way we can keep our land, make farms more fertile, buy more seed and become completely self-sufficient." ('Local food, global solution', *The Ecologist*, June 2002) But the question immediately forces itself upon us: how productive is the organic, diverse method of farming, traditionally practised by third world peasants, compared to industrial agriculture with its use of artificial fertilisers? Many observers of the hardships experienced by farmers of the underdeveloped world maintain that their productivity in terms of providing sufficient and healthy nourishment far outstrips the industrial method imposed by Western interests.

I want to quote from a report in *The Ecologist*, March 2003, 'The scarcity myth' by Frances Moore Lappé, an experienced observer of primitive agriculture:

> ... I learned that there is nothing natural about famine in today's world; that 'underdeveloped' is not an adjective but a verb, as Walter Rodney explained in his 1974 book *How Europe Underdeveloped Africa*.
>
> Fast forward to 2003. A buried *New York Times* story announces that 38 million people are at risk of starvation in Africa. The UN World Food Programme reports that demand for its aid is unprecedented. AIDS and government corruption are partly to blame, but the main culprit is drought.
>
> After three decades the message seems eerily familiar: scar-

city, caused by nature's vagaries and specific human frailties, is the culprit. Nothing appears to have changed. But appearances deceive. Much is changing. While the inertia of the old mindset still has us in its vice, an emergent map is bursting through in surprising places with remarkable rapidity ...

The dominant mindset tells us we're in a perpetual battle to overcome scarcity. Without capitalism's relentless drive, we'd probably all be going hungry by now.

In reality, however, it is this mindset that is propelling us to create the very scarcity we say we so fear. It was precisely to ring this alarm that I wrote *Diet for a Small Planet* 32 years ago. My message was that we humans were creating scarcity in so many different ways, including by turning livestock – ruminants whose genius is for manufacturing protein – into massive protein disposers.

For aeons ruminants had served humans by converting grass and other non-edibles into high-grade protein. Then, in just a blink of an eye, we'd come with concentrated grain feeding – industrial-style feedlots that in the US take 16 pounds of grain and soya and reduce them to one pound of food (in this case a cancer- and heart-disease-promoting steak).

Today, while hunger stunts the lives of hundreds of millions (people who are too poor to make a 'market demand' for the food they need), between a third and a half of all the world's grain goes to feed livestock. In the last three decades meat consumption even in low-income countries has doubled. It is the better-off who are creating this demand. Thirty years ago almost no grain went to livestock in China and Thailand, for example. Now over a quarter of grain consumption in these countries occurs in the production of meat.

With feedlot-fed cattle we also invented a superb system for squandering water: the production of just one US-style steer uses enough water to float a destroyer. This, in a world where millions go without clean water and groundwater tables are sinking on every continent.

In many ways, scarcity-creation has sped up. During WWII US Government posters advised: 'Eat fish, they feed themselves.' Now, four pounds of 'junk fish' like sardines (long a staple food of the poor) are turned into feed to produce just one pound of salmon. The latter is then priced out of the reach of the poor ...

Every species but ours has figured out how to feed itself and its offspring without destroying its life support. So, what's up with us? How could it be that we've created a system that destroys more than it creates? A system, what's more, that takes perfectly nutritious food and transforms it into a health hazard?

...

At the very same time, but unseen by most of us, a new and very different mindset is emerging. If you look, you can see it. But you have to really look. That's what my daughter Anna and I did when we wrote *Hope's Edge*. We travelled on five continents to nine countries. One was Kenya, where we talked with village women – members of Wangari Maathai's Green Belt Movement. These unschooled women are accomplishing what few would have considered possible. Confounding the scepticism of government foresters, they have created 6,000 co-operative tree nurseries throughout the country and planted 20 million trees.

Emboldened, Green Belters also began to question the impoverishing dependence on single exports like coffee (the producer prices of which have now hit an historic bottom). They began to re-learn the best of traditional farming practices and to reclaim lost crops. These activities yielded stronger community bonds, problem-solving groups, skills and enhanced food security.

...

Arriving in Brazil ... we were astonished to see ... the largest social movement in the hemisphere, and one that embodies not only a sophisticated critique of corporate globalisation but an alternative coming to life in thousands of communities across Brazil ... the Landless Worker's Movement (MST), a 20-year-old undertaking that has settled a quarter of a million families on 15 million acres of land throughout Brazil ...

Newly settled MST families told us that getting their own land was only a beginning. They had to consider all aspects of community-building, including the role of economic profit relative to other values ...

... Some MST farms, co-ops, and small businesses even sell internationally. But market exchange is counterbalanced by other values, with community solidarity and the health of the environment the most important. MSTers told us they were rejecting chemical agriculture not only because of the hazard to their own health (many had suffered pesticide poisoning as farm workers) but also out of concern that chemical residues might hurt the consumer.

146

A Brazilian research centre recently totalled the cost to the government of land reform. The figure included compensation for landowners, legal expenses and credit for new farmers. It then compared this figure with the cost of the number of people affected by land reform migrating to urban shanty towns instead. It turned out that the latter – the market's solution – would exceed in just one month the expense of an entire year of settling new farmers ...

We also visited Brazil's fourth largest city – Belo Horizonte. In 1993, its government had declared food a right of citizenship. This shift of thinking triggered dozens of innovations that have begun to end hunger in the city.

Little patches of city-owned land were made available at low rent to local organic farmers as long as they would keep prices within the reach of poor, inner-city dwellers. The city redirected the 13 cents provided by the federal government for each school child's lunch away from the purchase of corporate processed foods to buying local organic food instead. The result is enhanced children's nutritional intake ...

At the end of our stay in Belo Horizonte, we met Adriana Aranha, whose job in city government is to co-ordinate all these efforts. 'When you began,' I asked her, 'did you realise how much difference your efforts might make?' ...

... Aranha said, 'We had so much hunger in the world, but what is so upsetting, what I didn't know when I started this, is it's so easy to end it.' I've thought about that conversation many times since. Why was Aranha able to say 'It's easy'? I realise now that she is right if – only if – we can see with new eyes and free ourselves from the choking momentum of the inherited mental map. Then we can suddenly see new, more life-serving forms emerging.

These breakthroughs may be hard to detect – not only because the prevailing media doesn't cover them, but also because they do not constitute a new 'ism'. They don't add up to a new, packaged formula. They are – like Kenya's Green Belt Movement and the triumphs of Brazil's MST – about ordinary people trusting their deepest values as well as their common sense. In the process new mental maps emerge in which human beings are more than narrow consumers and democracy is more than a matter of pre-paid elections.

The prevailing mindset of Western capitalism which considers natural resources as a commodity to be exploited for profit must be made aware of its danger to human survival and of its responsibility to humanity. We need the political will to stop it exploiting the world's resources, and to share them with the world's population and to ensure the health of our planet. It is a moral and political transformation which is now required, as the old knee-jerk reactions of our culture are now outdated and counterproductive.

CHAPTER 10

The Politics of Global Sanity

The Failure of the United Nations Organisation.

In earlier chapters I suggested ways of dealing with capitalists by applying what may be called a radical compromise in limiting the harm they do to the natural environment and to the societies of the West. But the politics of capitalism is only one of the problems we are facing across the world. Many third world nations have acquired a certain amount of Western technology, partly to improve their production but also to improve their means of destruction. Some are now in possession of nuclear weaponry, and others, not quite as 'advanced' at the moment, possess biological and chemical poisons, supplied to them by industrialised nations for financial gain and to obtain much needed oil for their industries and to sustain their petrol guzzling way of life.

It is one of the paradoxes of history, or shall we say geology, that the deserts of the Middle East are the breeding ground of Islamic fanaticism. Saudi Arabia with 262 billion barrels and Iraq with 115 billion barrels of proven oil reserves are the largest source of oil in the world. The Western world needs a large part of that oil for its industry and wants to secure continued access to it. This is an obvious flash-point for international conflict, as everyone needs energy for industry and transportation. Islamic fanatics are outraged that Saudi Arabian rulers support the infidels of the West, and particularly the US, by providing an uninterrupted flow of oil, and make themselves fabulously rich in the process, and at the same time safeguard the stability of their regime against rebellion by Islamic fundamentalists.

The terrorists who attacked the World Trade Centre could hardly have anticipated that they would set off a chain reaction which has compromised the UN and NATO, and has shown up the disunity of the EU. The United Nations Organisation is in disarray over the Anglo-American war against Iraq to get rid of Saddam Hussein and his weapons of mass destruction. The organisations designed to safeguard peace in the world, for which millions have fought and died, have once again fallen victim to the re-emergence of national self-interest and religious fanaticism. The disunity of the United Nations and the divisions and rivalries in the EU and NATO have encouraged rogue countries to defy international rules for nuclear disarmament and control of nuclear and biochemical weapons.

It is well to remember that what we call politics is based upon the Athenian *polis* representing the forum of citizens united to affirm their ideas of freedom of self-expression and responsibility for the well-being of their community.

In retrospect we can now see that it was fairly simple in Athenian times to have a meeting-place, a parliament of people representing a community held together by shared traditions and values. The parliaments of Western democracy, having inherited the ideals of the *polis*, uphold freedom of speech and discussion, the virtues of rhetoric to defend the interests of the people they represent and what they think is good for their country. But how is one to apply these principles to the people across the globe? How can we proclaim the unity of mankind in the affirmation of the universal values of reason and democracy in view of the diversity of beliefs, traditions, religions and races which now more than ever divide mankind? And how is it possible to break through the barriers of prejudice and fanaticism and the ancient tribal and religious convictions in which people across the world are arrested?

Where is that voice of reason proclaiming man's innate capacity for truth and justice? Where are Plato, Socrates, Protagoras, Pericles and Aristotle, whose towering intellects have broken down the barriers which have perennially divided humanity into hostile camps fed by paranoid fears of the 'others' and their hostile and aggressive intentions? Even while we find ourselves in a global interdependence, we have no concept of universal values beyond the multitude of beliefs and national interests. We are on our guard against declarations of universal values after having had to endure the ideologies of communism, Nazism, nationalism, and even the market economy of capitalist consumerism which also claims to have universal validity, and we respond to the belief in the innate potentials of humanity with the cynicism of "human life being what it is – brutish, nasty and short" and there is nothing beyond, and we therefore have to look to our own advantage and if necessary fight for it.

Our 'scientific' philosophers can only observe the facts of human behaviour and its manifestations in the real world, and do their best to make us understand that there is nothing that transcends the human condition and our genetic inheritance (an increasingly fashionable theory that explains everything and guarantees a secure income for neuroscientists and drug manufacturers for many years to come). The truth is only what we can see around us and the facts we can observe. But the facts of human behaviour contradict our global responsibility.

In order to control the aggressive and warlike dispositions of nations, the League of Nations was founded, only to flounder in its inability to constrain those very dispositions among its member states. After the Second World War we tried again by creating the United Nations Organisation. It was a fine idea as people once more were determined to prevent wars, but its members were again a problem. While the nations of the world proclaimed their desire for peace and the prevention of wars, the UN became an organisation of convenience. Nations use it when they think that it will serve their interests, and avoid it when they see no likely gain for themselves. The self-serving interests of nations constantly override people's stated desires and aspirations for international friendship and co-operation while tribal, religious and racial instincts are embodied in the character of nation states. There are many large and small nations who consider themselves the representatives of their religious or economic beliefs and pay no heed to the call of international co-operation – unless it is on their terms.

It has often been said that the sovereignty of nations was the stumbling-block which defeated the League of Nations. We can see that this also applies to the efforts of the EU to secure the unity of nations in Europe by a supra-national system governed by Brussels, with its thousands of bureaucrats, experts and a multitude of legislation deemed necessary to harmonise and rationalise the running of the various member states and ultimately to create a United States of Europe. But they are dealing with ancient nations with their own traditions, history and strong sense of national identity and culture, proud of their right to govern and their own political establishments to administer their affairs. The megalomaniac ambitions of their presidents, chancellors or prime ministers disrupted the EU in the months leading up to the Iraq War. Blair wanted to lead Europe in co-operation with the United States, and Chirac, riding on the wave of anti-Americanism, proclaimed the reassertion of the glory of France, long overshadowed by the leading role of America in world affairs. This conflict has disrupted the EU as well as the United Nations Organisation and turned its major member states into hostile camps and its national leaders into adversaries.

Can the EU, the UN as well as NATO survive the damage they have inflicted upon themselves? And what kind of European and world organisation can be put in their place? But again, we have to consider not only the conflicting self-interests of the nations of Europe but also the conflict between the innumerable tribal and religious cultures across the world which defy all attempts to unify them in peaceful co-operation, both in spirit as well as in practice.

There are always megalomaniac individuals who are determined to be the leaders of their country's or religion's claim to supremacy and power – sadistic psychopaths who vent their pathologies upon the world by their single-minded, fanatical pursuit of power as a catharsis for their disturbed psyche. Many of them claim to speak in the name of God to give themselves unquestioned authority and power and to gain revenge for the psychological-narcissistic injuries they have suffered. There is, furthermore, the question why they are able to cause their fellow men to submit to their commands and to worship them. The most telling example was Saddam Hussein and his horrifying influence upon his country and upon the world.

152

The Psychopathology of a Tyrant.[1]

...

Dr Post, a qualified psychiatrist and professor at the George Washington University, pioneered the field of 'political psychology' during a 21-year career at the CIA.

Perhaps his most celebrated achievement was the profiling of Menachem Begin ('a detail person') and Anwar Sadat (a big-picture person') that helped President Jimmy Carter negotiate the Camp David peace treaty between Israel and Egypt. Over the years, he and his interdisciplinary team compiled many psychological profiles of leaders and militants for the US Government: all remain secret.

Though still a government consultant, Dr Post was already an academic when he first drafted his psychological portrait of Saddam Hussein after the Gulf War of 1991.

Since then, Saddam has beguiled the outside world with his protean talent for survival ...

According to Dr Post, Saddam's problems date back to his mother's pregnancy in Tikrit, about 100 miles (160km) north of Baghdad, in 1937. His father died in the fourth month of the pregnancy, probably of cancer. Then, in the seventh or eighth month, Saddam's 12-year-old brother also fell mortally ill.

Saddam's mother, Sabha, was predictably devastated and tried first to kill herself and then to abort her unborn child. Both times she was stopped by the intervention of well-to-do Jewish merchants who were family friends.

Baram, a professor at the University of Haifa and the author of a forthcoming biography of the Iraqi leader, has interviewed two surviving members of the Jewish family who saved Saddam ... [He reports:]

> ... They took her in the Mercedes to Baghdad. It took half a day. There they left her with the Baghdad branch of the family. These people lived very close to Baghdad's central hospital. They very quickly hospitalised the child.
>
> For four days, Sabha was sitting near her child [Saddam's brother] in bed. In the evening, she was going to the Jewish home. She spent the night there.
>
> On the fourth day, the doctors told her they would need to

153

operate on the child for a brain tumour. A woman from the Baghdad branch of the family, who was also pregnant, sat with Sabha
outside the room. Then the doctor told her the child had died on
the operating table.

It was then that Sabha tried to kill herself and abort Saddam.

The Jewish woman was taking her out of the hospital just across
the street to the Jewish home and Sabha threw herself under a bus.
She wanted to commit suicide ...

The Jewish woman managed to yank her out and saved her
life. Then she went home to the Jewish home and started beating
her belly against the door. She wanted to abort Saddam. She said:
"What will this child do for me? I have lost my husband."

She hated the embryo inside her.

[Dr Post continues:]

Again the Jewish family intervened, eventually sending her by
taxi back to Tikrit, where the other branch of the family kept a
watchful eye over her.

When Saddam was born on April 28, 1937, his mother shun-
ned him – a sign of deep depression. Her brother, Khayrallah
Talfah Msallat, Saddam's maternal uncle, took charge of the
child. It was only at the age of three that Saddam was reunited
with his mother, who had by then remarried to a distant relative
named Haj Ibrahim Hasan, with whom she had a daughter and
three more sons. The stepfather physically and psychologically
abused Saddam.

"He must have returned hoping at long last to be at the bos-
om of a warm and loving family and instead he was abused,"
Dr Post theorises. "People who are abused as children often
become abusive themselves, and he did it on a larger scene, a
national and regional scene. In Saddam's case, he has been able
to shape the social system so that it mirrors his own psychology. He has no father, and he then becomes father to his nation.
The sort of violence that was shown to him, he shows to the
people around him to keep them under control. He says: 'Never
again will I yield to superior force.' "

According to his semi-official biography, Saddam was so
impressed by the visit of a cousin who knew how to read and

write that, at the age of 10, he insisted that his family get him an education. When his mother and stepfather objected because there was no school in his village, Saddam left home in the middle of the night and returned to his uncle. This was a turning point for the boy, and for the Middle East.

Khayrallah, who was later to become governor of Baghdad, became not only Saddam's father figure but also his political mentor. He had fought in the Iraqi uprising against Britain in 1941 and spent five years in prison for his nationalist agitation. He told Saddam how his great-grandfather and two great uncles also gave their lives in the cause of Iraqi nationalism. The flavour of Khayrallah's political leanings can perhaps best be judged from the pamphlet that he wrote, and Saddam republished decades later. It was titled *Three Whom God Should Not Have Created: Persians, Jews and Flies.*

Dr Post believes Saddam's childhood tribulations created a common psychological condition called "the wounded self ". "In most people, this type of background would just be totally shattering – huge self-doubts, no sense of self-esteem, founded during the first few years of life," he says. "Saddam, however, went to his uncle's house, and his uncle filled him with dreams of glory and told him he had a major role to play in the history of Iraq."

Khayrallah told him tales of Nebuchadnezzar, the King of Babylon who conquered Jerusalem in 586 BC, and Saladin, the Muslim conqueror who evicted the Crusaders from Jerusalem in AD1187. And then, Gamel Abdel Nasser led the Free Officers' revolution in Egypt and became a hero in the Arab world by confronting Western imperialism. The Iraqi teenager had another hero to follow.

The noxious result was a syndrome Dr Post describes as "malignant narcissism".

"There are four components," he explains. "One, extreme grandiosity and self-absorption that mean you really do not empathise with the pain and suffering of others; two, a paranoid outlook, seeing yourself as surrounded by enemies, always on guard, not recognising your own role in creating it; three, no constraint of conscience; four, using whatever aggression is necessary to accomplish your goal. That is a very dangerous mixture."

So dangerous, in fact, that Dr Post is sketching out a new book to be called *Dreams of Glory: Narcissism in Politics*, with studies of fellow sufferers Fidel Castro, Osama bin Laden, Josef Stalin and Adolf Hitler.

For Dr Post, Saddam's psychological topography was perhaps best summarised in some architectural drawings of one of his palaces, which became public after the Gulf War. Beneath the gold and marble building lay a huge bunker of reinforced concrete, stocked with food and weapons. "It was a visual metaphor. Under this grandiose façade of arrogance, self-confidence and grandeur, you have the psychology of a siege state – insecure, on guard, ready to be attacked at all times," he observes. "That is his psychology, really. This arrogant façade sits astride a foundation of insecurity. That is very important." [2] ...

In his later years, particularly after 1991, Saddam claimed to be a direct descendant of Mohammed through the prophet's cousin, and gave himself divinely appointed authority and power. By speaking in the name of Allah, as revealed by Mohammed, he could do no wrong and convinced not only his fellow men but also himself of his omnipotence. We see here an example of manic compensation for a profound injury to his narcissistic needs combined with the sadistic urge to revenge himself upon the world and discharge his anger and rage upon it.

Saddam Hussein represents what I call the psychotic character which retains a measure of reasoning ability to serve and satisfy the maniacally inflated ego and find ways of discharging its sadistic urges. He will not stand alone against the world but divides it between 'we' and 'them', where 'we' incorporates relatives and those closely associated and blessed by their unquestioned submission to become part of his giant ego. They, 'the others', have to be tyrannised, tortured or killed in order to frighten them into submission and obedience. Even his victims, those whom he had tortured or killed, provide nourishment and evidence for his power.

Another example for this type of pathology is Osama bin Laden. I do not know enough about bin Laden's psychological development, and have to leave it to others like Dr Post, for instance, to clarify.

But the question still arises why people submit to such blood-thirsty tyrants and do their bidding despite everything. One can say that the utter conviction and unquestionable certainty which shows in their demeanour, the constant repetition of slogans known to their listeners from the Koran and therefore authenticated as holy script, has an hypnotic effect upon people not accustomed to rational discussion. This particularly applies to the followers of Islam with their worship of submission to the commands of Allah. The name Islam literally means submission, and through it they identify with their God; they let him enter into them and partake in his power. And they gain salvation and glory by fighting against the infidel and establishing the kingdom of Allah in the world. But, above all, it is the ability of those psychopathic maniacs to open the wounds of nations and religions defeated and insulted by the infidels, whose manic images of glory and superiority gives them the power to become leaders and tyrants in the name of the people who identify with the suffering endured by their hero and his passion for revenge.

Even nations who considered themselves civilised upholders of a great cultural heritage, become inflamed by fanatical hatred of those who they think have destroyed the pride of their country and 'poisoned the soul of their people.' We have seen this in Germany when millions followed Hitler in the war against the 'Jewish-Capitalist-Communist' enemies and acquiesced in the perpetration of the Holocaust and the killing of millions of their enemies.

We have seen this in the Soviet Union where Stalin became the great leader in the fight of the people, the workers and peasants oppressed and exploited by international capitalism, and in the endless wars between nations in Europe and tribes in Africa. People everywhere project their vanities, their urge for revenge, their desire to dominate, to acquire riches, to be admired and protected, upon their tribe or nation. As Plato said, what is not allowed to individuals is allowed to the state and acted out by it, not only with impunity but with the consent and the pride of the public.

How can one speak of 'united nations' when they were dis-united in the face of a bloodthirsty tyranny, with France and

Russia supplying Saddam Hussein with vast amounts of weaponry while presenting themselves as the champions of peace? What did they think the weapons would be used for but for the purpose of strengthening the tyrant's power to kill not only the Anglo-American alliance but also the millions of people of his own country who show the slightest sign of criticism towards his rule. The champions of peace, the faithful advocates of the United Nations Organisation encouraged the tyrant to do the killing on their behalf and received vast amounts of money from the oil revenues to pay for the weaponry they gave him.

One can only admire the unconscious wisdom of 'ordinary people', as for instance, when the cockneys call the making of a lot of money 'a killing' – unconscious memories of the tribal hunter who has to kill his prey in order to obtain the satisfaction of a good meal. In our civilised society the satisfaction of a good meal extends to the making of a huge amount of money. The French and the Russian oil companies supported by their governments were determined to prevent the downfall of Saddam Hussein's regime, with which they had made contracts for access to over 115 billion barrels of proven oil reserves, the largest in the world next to Saudi Arabia. And not only is the oil plentiful but it is also cheap to get out of the ground. The commercial and political battle to defeat the Anglo-American oil companies' claims to ownership of a major part of Iraq's oil continues, even after the war has ended with the military success of the Anglo-American alliance at the cost of disuniting the United Nations.

We cannot, however, advocate the abolition of the nation state in order to pave the way to global unity. Such a proposition would not only be rejected out of hand and considered as a kind of unrealistic fantasy, but would also ignore the role of a nation to bring a semblance of unity to the diverse beliefs, religions, ideologies and interests of its citizens, upheld with varying degrees of determination or fanaticism. It decides upon the laws of the country and ensures their implementation by the law courts and the police, it administers the system of education, transport, electricity and power, as well as the economic system, and protects in some measure those who for various reasons are unable to look after themselves through disability, unemployment and poverty; it has to provide for a wide range of social services.

But, as we have seen, nations lack the capacity for international co-operation and the creation of the global unity of mankind. They do not uphold a universal purpose which unites the nations and serves humanity in the pursuit of peace, the protection of nature and the biosphere and the protection of humanity from its aggressive and destructive drives which have pervaded the history of nations, now made immeasurably more dangerous by modern science and technology. Science can be of immense benefit for the improvement of life, of man and of nature, but can also enhance immeasurably mankind's powers of destruction.

There are now approximately 110 nations in the world and countless tribes and religions, each determined to increase their power and promote their own aims. Some of the most extreme and fanatical amongst them have taken over the government of their nations, as has happened in Iraq as well as in North Korea where they ruthlessly enforce nationalistic feelings amongst its people to promote a Stalinist type of dictatorship and the acquisition of nuclear weaponry. In Zimbabwe, Mugabe has established himself as the advocate of racism, in order to rid the country of its white farmers in the name of the people's liberation. There are many other countries in Africa and Asia where tribal and religious fanatics have gained a dominant influence. While most of the nations of the world manage to contain and control their extremist groups, many have become their victims.

We can see our planet as a spaceship that travels through space and time in its journey through the galaxy. Its passengers have to be fully aware of the need to maintain its safety. If however they start fighting amongst each other and allow infantile tantrums of rage and destruction to get the better of them, they are likely to damage it, and it will get out of control, and fall down. It would be the end of the journey of our planet, the end of its history and of life upon it, unless we can be transferred to another spaceship, as some fantasts have thought, but this is exceedingly unlikely to happen. Whatever the differences between the passengers, their overriding concern must be the safety of their spaceship.

In an organisation for global sanity we have to convince the nations of the world of their collective responsibility for the safety of our planet and for the further existence and development of mankind. While we differ in our cultures and races and religions, we are all united in our responsibility to protect the life of this planet, the only home we have in the vast universe.

A World Organisation for Global Sanity

It is a matter of common sense that we must make every effort to overcome the limitation of nation states and direct their attention to the interests of humanity beyond the imperatives of national self-interest and create a world organisation for the protection of nature and the protection of mankind from its destructive drives. And we need a vision of a healthy planet and a healthy and sane humanity to encourage us to take practical steps towards it, and to believe that it is possible to do so. The nations of the world must be given the opportunity to discuss openly and honestly how they can find agreement and unity on the most important issues facing mankind now.

The World Organisation for Global Sanity will have three interacting sections:

1) a Legislative Chamber, in other words, a World Parliament;

2) an Executive Chamber; and

3) an Advisory Council to focus our attention on the ideals and purposes of the World Organisation, and to discuss and advise upon policies for promoting the unity of mankind in its pursuit of peace and co-operation. Its first task should be a declaration of aims proclaiming the vision for a united and sane humanity worthy of its innate potentials, and also to advise what needs to be done in practical terms, and ensure that nations cease to be focussed upon the promotion of their self-interest but that nations serve humanity.

In Plato's terms, the Advisory Council and its Proclamation of Aims would act as the philosophers who free mankind from the illusions of the cave, which in our time is represented by the mindset of the nations' self-interest, and lead us to the open, sun-lit clarity of truth, beauty and justice, and the love of life. Plato's philosophers would in our modern world include scientists, psychoanalysts, neurologists, economists, writers and intellectuals as well as politicians, who are convinced of the validity of this project and are enthusiastic to participate in its realisation. The first step therefore will be to find a number of people of good will ready to join the Advisory Council and prepare the Proclamation of Aims for the future of humanity.

I do not wish here to compose this Proclamation of Aims, as I do not want to anticipate the discussions and arguments among people who are keen to participate and express their views in the creation of a new world order. I would, however, suggest the establishment of a World Parliament comprising about 110 nation states who would be invited to join it. They would be given the Proclamation of Aims and if persuaded by its arguments would be asked to support the establishment of a World Parliament and to participate in it.

The World Parliament

The legislature of the World Parliament would have the task of translating the aims of the Proclamation into laws, ensuring the peaceful co-operation of the nations of the world. The Executive Chamber of the Parliament of nations would determine what actions have to be taken to carry out the laws arrived at by the Legislative Chamber. This is in accordance with the majority of state parliaments, and it would be first of all concerned with the co-operation of nations and would refrain from interfering or intruding upon the domestic affairs of nations which would be considered the responsibility of their own elected government. However, the World Parliament should have the right to discuss and consider the desirability of co-operative forms of production of skilled and intelligent workers and their ownership of tools and machinery, and the aims of education and the role of capitalists in their society. The national parliaments, however, would have the duty to discuss the ecological problems of this planet and make laws to protect the natural environment.

The Proclamation of Aims of the 'World Organisation for Global Sanity' and for the establishment of a World Parliament would be presented to all the nation states of the world, and they would be asked to sign it as a declaration of their agreement with its aims and their willingness to participate in the world-wide effort towards its realisation.

The World Parliament would not replace the parliaments of nation states or intrude in their policy-making; the global parliament would be called upon to make a wide range of propositions and rules and present them to the national parliaments which would then debate those propositions and turn them into laws if their elected members decide to do so.

But then there arises the question how the members of the World Parliament would be elected and by whom. As national parliaments extend their deliberations from the affairs of their nation to the promotion of the welfare and security of the planet both on the ecological as well as human level, they would be asked to nominate two prominent individuals of their country whom they consider most suitable, or two of their MPs, to be permanent members of the World Parliament. Being elected by the world's nation states, they would represent the majority of the world's population and actively participate in making political and economic decisions which are necessary to overcome the problems and dangers facing humanity. There would be a shift away from 'us against them' in the recognition that we are together in our responsibility for the life and well-being of our planet.

If we consider that the average population of each of the 110 nation states is about 40–50 million people, then the two representatives of each nation would represent about 5,000,000,000 people of the world. Countries which have a parliamentary democracy may decide to call an election to test the public's desire for a World Parliament and to participate in it. There would be public meetings and discussions on the issue, and those in favour would be free to propagate their beliefs.

Indeed, it would herald the age of consent, passionately advocated by George Monbiot (*The Age of Consent*, 2003). In his book, he argues the case for a world government and describes in detail the problems facing the people of the world to make their voices heard. He proposes a series of 'global meetings' open to everyone and organised by the 'World Social Forum' where thousands of people are already participating. This, he says, is the biggest of the global justice movements' gatherings and in 2003 over 100,000 people took part. He also advocates public protest demonstrations in the streets of the big towns to further their cause, but the trouble is that whenever they were held they tended to end up in violence and destruction. Rather than convert people to their cause, the public is becoming resentful about 'just another public disturbance one has to put up with in our age of violence'. And in any case, the number of people engaged in their gatherings and demonstrations were infinitesimal in relation to the world population.

Of course we cannot expect that every nation state would want to participate in the World Parliament, but if in the near future 40 or 50 national governments agree to sign the Proclamation of Aims it would be a great step forward for humanity. It would mean that something like 2,500,000,000 people across the world declare their commitment towards making a new world order to affirm and safeguard the life of our planet and avoid the drift to mankind's self-destruction, to regain a vision of the future and take steps to create it.

Democratic societies sympathetic towards a World Parliament would not have to fear a revolution which would endanger their democratic institutions, as the economic and political transformation involved would chiefly apply to the underdeveloped areas of the world and also be of benefit to their own country. Whether people wish to form a political party devoted to a social democracy as outlined earlier is up to the voters and can be done by democratic means.

The advocates of a World Parliament in countries sympathetic to its ideas would have their newspapers and journals propagating and explaining it to the public; they could have houses for public meetings and lectures; its ideas would be taught in schools and even university courses, with degrees in the psychology and ethics of a global society.

The current sense of intellectual and moral stagnation would give way to a new optimism, and the frustrated and repressed desire for justice and consideration for our fellow men could begin to express itself openly and with new confidence. We all need the reassurance of 'official' support – the encouragement of the good superego – for our intellectual and moral aspirations, to make us feel that something which appeared impossible can now be done. We can begin to discuss and debate the big issues without becoming angry and aggressive.

There could be films showing the hero preventing a war by managing to get the World Parliament to exercise its powers to achieve peaceful solutions. This would not only be an exciting piece of propaganda but would also show how the World Parliament would operate.

People would feel their sense of responsibility and a sense of pride to be active agents in the creation of a new future.

Politicians never had as great a duty to act responsibly, and this also applies to leaders of religions. One should, therefore, send the Proclamation of Aims to the leaders of the major religions, hoping that the blessing it will bring to humanity and to life, which God has created, would make them think and re-think some of their dogmas.

But what can one do with the extreme fundamentalist religions and their fanatical leaders who preach and proclaim *jihad*, the holy war against the infidel, Americans, Europeans and the Jews? First of all one should remind them of the teaching of the religion of Abraham, whose descendants they claim to be. The most important of its commandments is: Do not do unto others what you don't want them to do to you. This is the foundation and sum of the spirit of Abraham's religion proclaimed by the prophets, and should be taught again, now more than ever, in our time:

Worship life and do not preach death, for this betrays God's love for his creation. Only Eros can vanquish Thanatos.

Notes and References

PROLOGUE

[1] (p. x): Stalinism can be considered a counter-revolution against Lenin's optimistic belief in the power of the international working class to create a socialist society, which Stalin thought was only possible by coercion. Russia, which did not have a well established capitalist bourgeoisie and was still dominated by the feudal regime of Czarism, underwent a feudal counter-revolution resurrected by Stalin's form of dictatorship. It was not a counter-revolution of the bourgeoisie but of feudalism.

[2] (p. xv): See *International Journal of Psychoanalysis* overview: 'In this Issue ... Volume 82–Part 4–2001', second paragraph.

CHAPTER 1

[1] (p. 15): The development of the race relations industry, which in America is still funded, is closely described in the book by Dinesh de Souza: *The End of Racism*: Principles for a Multiracial Society, The Free Press, London 1995.

CHAPTER 2

(p. 19): [1]Winnicott [1957]; [2]Graves [1989]; [3]Teresa Cottrell; [4]Fedor-Freybergh [2000]. These four quotes are taken from Chapter 3 –'The psychological impact of being born too soon'– of an as yet unpublished dissertation by Teresa A. Cottrell.

(p. 20): [5]Verny [1982]; [6] Winnicott [1986]. From line 16 to line 6, p. 23, text selected from Teresa Cottrell's thesis.

(p. 21): [7]Schore [1999]; [8] Schore [1996]; [9]Trevarthen [1996]; [10] Cottrell, Ch. 3–Section 2 *The prenatal scene.* [11]*ibid* Cottrell.

(p. 22): [12]Cottrell; [13] Brazelton and Cramer [1991], from Cottrell: Ch. 3–Section 2 *The postnatal scene.*

(pp. 22–23): [14]Winnicott [1965] and [1956]. [15]Bowlby [1985].

CHAPTER 3

[1] (pp. 49–50): The last paragraph on p. 49 and the first paragraph on p. 50, as indicated, are taken from an article by Patience Wheatcroft: 'Sharpen your axes shareholders, heads must roll at Marconi tomorrow'; Comment; Opinion; *The Times* 17 July 2001.

[2] (p. 58): Matthew Taylor, Social Commentator: 'What fathers really need to teach sons', *The Evening Standard*, Friday 9th August 2002.

[3] (p. 62): Thursday 9 August 2001, Times2, p. 2. 'Three cheers for chauvinism'; Cover story by Michael Gove.

[4] (p. 62–63): *The Times* Thursday 28 March 2002, page 26. 'What the world needs now is economists'; Comment; Opinion; by Anatole Kaletsky.

CHAPTER 6

[1] (p. 81): Jean Gerson: *Contra vanam curiositatem*, Opera omnia, Vol. 1., ed. L. Ellies du Pin, 1728, 5 vols.

[2] (p. 81): Johan Huizinga: *The Waning of the Middle Age*s, Chapter 14, p. 187, Penguin Books, 1972.

[3] (p. 82): Jan van Ruysbroeck: *The Mirror of Eternal Salvation*, Werken, Vol. 2, Brussels.

[4] (p. 82): Johan Huizinga: *The Waning of the Middle Age*s, Chapter 14, p. 191, Penguin, 1972.

[5] (p. 83): Burckhardt, J: *The Civilisation of the Renaissance in Italy*, Penguin, 1990.

CHAPTER 7

[1] (p. 95): Richard Sheppard: *In Search of the Unique*, RIBA, 1973.

[2] (p. 95): Malcolm MacEwen: *Crisis in Architecture*, RIBA, 1974.

[3] (p. 96): C. A. Doxiades: *Anthropocosmos* – The World of Man, Aspen Institute for Humanistic Studies, 1966.

[4] (p. 96): *ibid.*

[5] (p. 98): A. Sant'Elia and F. Marinetti: *The Futuristic Manifesto.*

[6] (p. 98): *ibid.*

[7] (p. 99): Peter Hall, *New Society*, October 1968.

[8] (pp. 99–100): 'Norman's Conquest' by Rowan Moore. This is an extract of an article published in the March 2002 issue of *Prospect*. To read it in full visit www.prospect-magazine.co.uk

[9] (p. 104): Front page headline from the *Evening Standard*, 17th June 2003.

[10] (p. 107): 'Foster show reaches for the sky', Marcus Binney, Architecture Correspondent, *The Times*, Saturday 31 May 2003, p.45).

CHAPTER 8

[1] (p. 115): 'Sustainable development is a hoax: we cannot have it all' – Unlimited desire is bound to destroy a world of limited resources, by Jeremy Seabrook: *The Guardian*, Monday 5 August, 2002). © Jeremy Seabrook.

[2] (p. 117): 'In an interview with *The Sunday Telegraph*, David Bell, the head of Ofsted, said that too many children were receiving a "disrupted and dishevelled" upbringing. As a result the verbal and behavioural skills of the nation's five-year-olds were at an all-time low, causing severe difficulties for schools.

'Mr Bell said that one of the key causes was the failure of parents to impose proper discipline at home, which led to poor behaviour in class. Another serious concern was the tendency to sit children in front of the television, rather than talking and playing with them. This meant that many were unable to speak properly when they started school ...

"There is evidence that children's verbal skills are lacking. We should encourage parents to talk to their children and give them a whole range of stimulating things to do and not just assume that the television, or whatever, will do all that for them." ...

'Monica Galt, the head teacher of King's Road primary school in Manchester, said that many children started school with minimum social skills: "... Some children have never sat at a table because their parents let them eat their tea sitting on the floor in front of the television." ' (Julie Henry, Education Correspondent, 'Ofsted head says that five-year-olds led 'disrupted and dishevelled lives', *The Sunday Telegraph*, 31 August 2003).

[3] (p. 117): From the introduction by Ivo Mosley to *Dumbing Down* – culture, politics and the mass media. Edited by Ivo Mosley, Imprint Academic, 2000. The complete paragraph reads: "Never before in human history has so much cleverness been used to such stupid ends. The cleverness is in the creation and mani-

pulation of markets, media and power; the stupid ends are in the destruction of community, responsibility, morality, art, religion and the natural world."

[4] (pp. 123–124): 'Creaking public service now staggers along on grey power', Jill Sherman, Whitehall editor, Home News, *The Times*, 3 September 2002.

[5] (pp. 129–130): 'Has the Left learnt nothing from the past 30 years?' by Anthony Hilton, *Evening Standard*, 22 June 2003.

CHAPTER 9

[1] (p. 137): See article 'State of the Planet' by Matilda Lee, p. 6. This article first appeared in the September 2002 edition of the *The Ecologist*. www.theecologist.org

[2] (p. 140): According to the Office of National Statistics, 1,000 farmers and farm workers are leaving the land in Britain each week – 52,000 for the whole of 2002.

Having encouraged and financed the export of cheap 'luxury' food from the underdeveloped countries into the West, Western farmers cannot compete with the cheap imports, and have to be subsidised by their governments. In the EU, this means that European countries and in particular, England, have to pay large sums to keep French farmers and, to some smaller extent, British farmers, in existence, and even so Britain is losing its farmers and British agriculture becomes non viable.

[3] (p. 142): The environmental facts and figures on this page are gleaned from the article 'State of the Planet' by Matilda Lee, *The Ecologist*, September 2002, pp. 6–11. See Note [1] above, (p. 137).

CHAPTER 10

[1] (pp. 153–156): These pages are taken from James Bone's interview with Dr Post, *The Times*, T2 February 28, 2003, 'Saddam: Why I blame his mother'; Interview; Jerrold Post; James Bone. A psychiatric expert on Saddam Hussein tells James Bone that the childhood trauma of rejection by his mother turned the Iraqi leader into a murderous tyrant – and that he owes his life to the intervention of a Jewish family.

[2] (p. 156): End of citations from James Bone's interview with Dr Post.

Bibliography

Abraham, Karl: *A Short Study in the Development of the Libido,* Hogarth Press, 1927.

— *Selected Papers on Psychoanalysis*, Karnac Books, 1988.

Adler, Alfred: *The Education of Children.* Translated by Eleanore and Friedrich Jensen, G. Allen & Unwin, London 1930.

— *Guiding the Child on the Principles of Individual Psychology.* Translated by Benjamin Ginzburg, G. Allen & Unwin, London 1930.

— *Social Interest: Adler's Key to the Meaning of Life*, Oneworld, 1998.

Adorno, T. et al: *The Authoritarian Personality*, Norton, 1982.

Adorno, T. and Horkheimer, M: *Aspects of Sociology*, London, 1979.

— *Dialectic of Enlightenment*, Allen Lane, 1973.

Alexander, Franz: *Psychoanalysis and Psychotherapy*, George Allen & Unwin, 1957.

Applebaum, Anne: *Gulag: History of the Soviet Camps*, Doubleday, 2003.

Bauer, Otto (1881–1938): *Faschismus und Kapitalismus*, edited by Wolfgang Abendroth, Europa Verlag, Vienna, 1968.

— *The Question of Nationalities and Social Democracy.* Translated by Joseph O'Donnell, London, 2000.

— *Austrian Democracy under Fire*, Labour Publications Department, London 1934.

— *The Austrian Revolution.* Translated by H. J. Stenning, Leonard Parsons, London 1925.

Bernfeld, S: *Psychology of the Infant*, Kegan Paul, 1929.

— 'Sigmund Freud', *International Journal of Psychoanalysis*, 1951.

Bornemann, Ernest (ed.): *The Psychoanalysis of Money*, Urizen Books, 1976.

Bowlby, J: *Attachment and Loss,* Vol. 1. *Attachment*, Hogarth Press, 1969.

— *Attachment and Loss,* Vol. 2. *Separation, Anxiety and Anger*, 1973.

— *Attachment and Loss,* Vol. 3. *Loss, Sadness and Depression*, 1980.

Brown, N. O: *Life against Death: The Psychoanalytic Meaning of History*, Routledge & Kegan Paul, 1959.

Burckhardt, J: *The Civilisation of the Renaissance in Italy*, Penguin, 1990.

Childe, V. G: *Man Makes Himself*, Watts, 1936.

Clark, Grahame: *World Prehistory*, CUP, 1969.

Cohn, Norman: *Warrant for Genocide*, Serif, 1996.

Corbusier, Le: *Vers Une Architecture*. Paris: Editions Crès, 1923. Translated from the French by Frederick Etchells and published as *Towards a New Architecture*, London, The Architectural Press, 1927.

Damasio, Antonio: *The Feeling of What Happens*, Heinemann, 2000.

— *Looking for Spinoza: Joy, Sorrow and the Feeling Brain*, Heinemann, 2003.

Deleuze, G. and Guattari, F: *Anti-Oedipus: Capitalism and Schizophrenia*, Athlone Press, 1984.

Deutsch, Helene: *The Psychology of Female Sexuality*, 1925.

— *The Psychology of Women, Vol 2.*, Grune & Stratton, 1945.

Deutscher, I: *Stalin: A Political Biography*, Oxford University Press, 1949.

Ditfurth, Hoimar von : *Der Geist fiel nicht vom Himmel*, Dtv, 1991.

Dobb, M: *Studies in the Development of Capitalism*, Routledge, 1963.

Doxiadis, C. A: *Anthropocosmos, the World of Man*, Aspen Institute for Humanistic Studies, 1966.

Eaton, Ruth: *Ideal Cities: Utopianism and the (Un)Built Environment*, Thames & Hudson, 2002.

Einstein, A. & Freud, S: *Why War?* 1933.

Ellenberger, H. F: *The Discovery of the Unconscious – The History and Evolution of Dynamic Psychiatry*, Allen Lane, 1970.

Ellul, Jacques: *The Technological Society*, Random House, 1967.

Erikson, E. H: *Childhood and Society*, Vintage, 1995.

— *Identity: Youth and Crisis*, Faber, 1971.

Fedor-Freybergh, P. and Vogel, V. M. L (eds): *Prenatal and Perinatal Psychology and Medicine: A Comprehensive Survey of Research and Practice*, Parthenon, 1988.

Fenichel, O: *The Psychoanalytic Theory of Neurosis*, Routledge, 1996.

— 'A Critique of the Death Instinct', in *Collected Papers*, Routledge & Kegan Paul, 1954.

Ferenczi, S: *First Contributions to Psychoanalysis*, Hogarth, 1955.

— *Further Contributions to the Theory and Technique of Psycho-analysis*, Karnac Books, 1994.

Frankl, George: *The End of War or the End of Mankind*, Globe Publications, 1955.

— *The Failure of the Sexual Revolution*, Kahn & Averill, 1974; Nel Mentor Classics, 1975, Open Gate Press, 2004.

— *The Social History of the Unconscious – A Psychoanalysis of Society*, Open Gate Press, 1990, 2002. Available in two volumes as:
— *Archaeology of the Mind*, Open Gate Press, 1992.
— *Civilisation: Utopia and Tragedy*, Open Gate Press, 1992.

— *The Unknown Self*, Open Gate Press, 1990, 1993, 2001.

— *Exploring the Unconscious*, Open Gate Press, 1994, 2001.

— *Foundations of Morality*, Open Gate Press, 2000, 2001.

Freud, Anna: *The Ego and the Mechanisms of Defence*, Hogarth Press, 1937.

Freud, Sigmund: 1900 *The Interpretation of Dreams*, S.E. Vol. 4–5.

— 1905 *Three Essays on the Theory of Sexuality*, S.E. Vol. 7.

— 1908 *Character and Anal Eroticism*, S.E. Vol. 9.

— 1913 *Totem and Taboo*, S.E. Vol. 13.

— 1914 *On Narcissism*, S.E. Vol. 14.

— 1915 *The Unconscious*, S.E. Vol. 14.

— 1915–17 *Introductory Lectures on Psychoanalysis*, S.E. Vol. 15–16.

— 1920 *Beyond the Pleasure Principle*, S.E. Vol. 18.

— 1921 *Group Psychology and the Analysis of the Ego*, S.E. Vol. 18.

— 1923 *The Ego and the Id*, S.E. Vol. 19.

— 1927 *The Future of an Illusion*, S.E. Vol. 21.

— 1930 *Civilization and its Discontents*, S.E. Vol. 21.

— 1933 *New Introductory Lectures on Psychoanalysis*, S.E. Vol. 22.

— 1938 *An Outline of Psychoanalysis*, S.E. Vol. 23.

Fromm, Erich: *Escape from Freedom*, Holt, Rinehart & Winston, 1941.

— *Psychoanalysis and Religion*, Yale University Press, 1950.

— *The Sane Society*, Routledge, 1956.

— *The Revolution of Hope*, Harper & Row, 1970.

— *The Crisis of Psychoanalysis*, Jonathan Cape, 1971.

— *The Anatomy of Human Destructiveness*, Penguin, 1977.

Glover, Edward: *On the Early Development of Mind*, Allen & Unwin, 1956.

— *The Birth of the Ego*, Allen & Unwin, 1968.

Goldman, Lucien: *The Human Sciences and Psychology*, Jonathan Cape, 1969.

Gould, Stephen Jay: *Ontogeny and Phylogeny*, Harvard University Press, 1985.

Greer, Germaine: *The Female Eunuch*, Paladin, 1971.

Groddeck, Georg: *The Book of the It*, Vision Press, 1961.

Guntrip, Harry: *Personality Structure and Human Interaction*, Karnac Books, 1995.

— *Schizoid Phenomena, Object Relations and the Self*, Hogarth Press, 1968.

Harth, Erich: *Windows on the Mind: Reflections on the Principal Basis of Consciousness*, Harvester Press, 1982.

Horkheimer, Max, ed: *Studien über Autorität und Familie*, Paris, 1936.

Huxley, Julian: *The Uniqueness of Man*, Chatto & Windus, 1941.

— *Evolution, The Modern Synthesis*, George Allen & Unwin, 1942.

Jahoda, M: 'Social Psychology and Psychoanalysis', *Bulletin of the British Psychological Society*, 25, pp. 269–274.

James, William: *The Varieties of Religious Experience*, Fontana Library, 5th Impression, 1971.

Jung, C. G: *Symbols of Transformation*, Routledge, 1956.

— *On the Psychology of the Unconscious*, Collected Works, Vol. 8, 1953.

— *Modern Man in Search of a Soul*, Ark Paperbacks, 1984.

Kardiner, A: *The Individual and His Society*, Columbia University Press, 1939.

Klein, Melanie: *Contributions to Psychoanalysis*, Hogarth Press, 1948.

— *The Psychoanalysis of Children*, Virago, 1989.

— *Envy and Gratitude*, Hogarth Press, 1975.

Koestler, A: *The Ghost in the Machine*, Hutchinson, 1967.

Koestler, A, et al: *The God that Failed*, Bantam Books, 1970.

Kohut, H: *The Analysis of the Self*, Hogarth, for the Institute of Psychoanalysis, 1971.

Laing, R.D: *The Divided Self*, Penguin, 1975.

Laqueur, Walter: *No End to War: Terrorism in the Twenty-First Century*, Continuum, 2003.

Lasch, Christopher: *The Culture of Narcissism*, Abacus, 1980.

LeDoux, Joseph: *The Emotional Brain: The Mysterious Underpinnings of Emotional Life*, Weidenfeld & Nicolson, 1998.

Lens, Sidney: *The Military Industrial Complex*, Kahn & Averill, 1971.

MacEwen, Malcolm: *Crisis in Architecture*. London, RIBA Publications, 1974.

Manser, Jose: *Hugh Casson: A Biography*, 2000.

Marcuse, Herbert: *One Dimensional Man*, Routledge, 1991.

— *Eros and Civilization*, Ark, 1987.

Marinetti, F. T: 'The Founding and Manifesto of Futurism', in *Le Figaro*, February 20, 1909.

Marx, Karl: *Economic and Philosophical Manuscripts of 1844*, Lawrence & Wishart, The Collected Works in Fifty Volumes.

— *Capital. A Critique of Political Economy*, 1877. London, Lawrence & Wishart. The Collected Works in Fifty Volumes.

— *Grundrisse*, Penguin in association with New Left Review, 1973.

— and Engels, F: *The Communist Manifesto*, Penguin, 1967.

Mead, Margaret: *Coming of Age in Samoa*, Penguin, 1977.

Mitchell, J: *Psychoanalysis and Feminism,* Penguin, 2000.

Monbiot, George: *The Age of Consent*, Flamingo–HarperCollins, 2003.

Nietzsche, Friedrich: *Morgenröte [Daybreak]*, 1881.

Parsons, T: *Social Structure and Personality*, The Free Press, 1970.

Pevsner, Nicholas: *Pioneers of Modern Design: From William Morris to Walter Gropius.* Penguin, Harmondsworth, 1988.

Piaget, J: *Origins of Intelligence in Children*, International Universities Press, 1992.

Popper, K: *Conjectures and Refutations*, Routledge & Kegan Paul, 1969.

Rees, Martin: *Our Final Century*, Heinemann, 2003.

Reich, Wilhelm: *Character Analysis*, Vision Press, 1951.

— *The Mass Psychology of Fascism*, Penguin, 1983.

— *The Sexual Revolution*, Vision Press, 1972.

Reik, Theodor: *The Unknown Murderer,* Hogarth Press, 1936.

— *Ritual – Psychoanalytic Studies*, Farrar, Strauss, 1957.

— *Masochism in Modern Man*, Souvenir Press, 1975.

Riesman, D: *The Lonely Crowd*, Yale University Press, 1961.

Roheim, Geza: *Psychoanalysis and Anthropology*, International Universities Press, 1971.

Rorvik, D: *As Man Becomes a Machine*, Souvenir Press, 1973.

Roszak, T: *The Making of a Counter Culture*, University of California Press, 1995.

Sant'Elia, A: *Manifesto of Futurist Architecture.* Lacerba, Florence, 1914.

Sant'Elia, A. and Marinetti, F. T: 'The Futuristic Manifesto' 1914.

Schore, A. N: [1996] The experience-dependent maturation of a regulatory system in the orbital prefrontal cortex and the origin of developmental psychopathology. *Development and Psychopathology*, 8: 59–87.

Schrödinger, E: *What Is Life? – The Physical Aspect of the Living Cell.* With *Mind and Matter* and *Autobiographical Sketch*, CUP, 1992.

Sharp, Dennis, et al: *Twentieth-century Classics: by Walter Gropius, Le Corbusier and Louis Khan: Bauhaus, Dessau, 1925–6; Unité d'Habitation, Marseilles 1945–52; Salk Institute, La Jolla, California 1959–60.* Phaidon, 1999.

Simmel, Georg: *The Philosophy of Money*, Routledge, 1990.

Smith, Adam: *The Wealth of Nations*, Modern Library Edition.

Sorokin, P: *Society, Culture and Personality: Their Structure and Dynamics*, Harper's Social Studies Series, 1947.

Stekel, W: *Sadism and Masochism*, Liveright Publ. Co., 1939.

— *Patterns of Psychosexual Infantilism*, Peter Nevill, 1953.

Strachey, A: *The Unconscious Motives of War*, Allen & Unwin, 1957.

Sterba, R: *Introduction to the Psychoanalytic Theory of the Libido*, Robert Brunner, Inc., 1968.

Sulloway, F: *Freud, Biologist of the Mind*, Harvard University Press, 1992.

Sweezy, P. M: *The Theory of Capitalist Development*, Modern Readers Paperback, 1970.

Tawney, R. H: *Religion and the Rise of Capitalism*, Pelican, 1940.

Trevarthen, C: *First Impulses for Communication: Negotiating Meaning and Moral Sentiments with Infants*, 1996.

Verny, Thomas: *The Secret Life of the Unborn Child*, 1982.

Weber, Max: *The Protestant Ethic and the Spirit of Capitalism*, Routledge, 1992.

Weinstock, M: 'Does Prenatal Stress Impair Coping and Regulation of Hypethalamic-Pituitary-Adrenal Axis?' *Neuroscience & Biobehavioral Reviews,* 21, 1 (1997), pp. 1–10.

Wells, H. G: *The Mind at the End of Its Tether*, Heinemann, 1945.

Wheen, Francis: *Karl Marx*, Fourth Estate, 1999.

Winnicott, D. W: *Collected Papers*, Tavistock Publications, 1958.

— *The Maturational Process and the Facilitating Environment*. Studies in the Theory of Emotional Development, Hogarth, 1965.

— *The Family and Individual Development*, Tavistock Publications, 1965.

Zweig, Stefan: *The World of Yesterday*, University of Nebraska Press, 1964.

Index

97, 102, 103, 110, 135, 151
— impulse-dominated behaviour
48
Berlin, Isaiah 85
Binney, Marcus 107
Biosphere 15, 17, 93, 94, 135,
136, 159
Blair, Tony 62, 152
Body 3, 4, 23
— body contact 27, 28, 30, 34
— body periphery 20, 27, 34, 35
Bourgeoisie x, 48, 166
Bowlby, John 23
Brain xvi, 3, 9, 17, 18, 21, 23,
25, 26, 51, 56, 70, 109
— cortex xvi, 70
— frontal lobes 9, 18, 48, 70
— prefrontal lobes 9, 34
Brazelton, T. B. 22
Brazil 146–147
— Belo Horizonte 147
— Landless Worker's Movement
146, 147
Breast 24, 31, 35, 61
Brussels 152
Buchenwald xiv
Buffett, Warren 132
Bulimia 51
— shopping bulimia 128
Burckhardt, J. 83
Bureaucracy 60, 101, 102, 107,
124, 125, 126, 152
Bush the Elder, George 115
Bush the Younger, George 115

C
Camus, Albert 28
Capital 71, 73, 101, 119, 120,
128, 129, 130
— fixed capital 123
— social capital 118, 123
Capitalism x, xvii, 11, 37, 51, 61,
74, 76, 130, 132, 133, 143, 145,

148, 149, 157
— casino of capitalism 119, 120,
127, 128, 129, 132
Capitalist(s) 8, 11, 12, 19, 20, 37,
46, 50, 51, 59, 62, 63, 71, 75,
101, 102, 118, 120, 127, 128,
131, 138, 161, 166
— capitalist democracy 11, 19,
28, 116
Carter, President Jimmy 153
Casson, Sir Hugh 95
Castro, Fidel 156
Catatonia 6
Catharsis 152
Catholic Church xi, 79, 80, 81,
82
causa prima 90
Character formation xiii, xiv, 19,
26, 31, 34, 42, 103, 104, 105,
114, 115
Charlemagne 80
Charles, Prince of Wales 100
China 106–107, 145
Chirac, Jacques 152
Christ 80, 81, 82
Christianity 10, 54, 80, 82
— Christian(s) 38, 80
— the Cross 80, 81
City 69, 92, 93, 96, 98, 99, 110–
113
— as a symbol of man 110–111
Civilisation xv, 47, 48, 57, 84,
86, 115, 136
— the cradle of civilisation 115
— Western civilisation xvii, 7, 8,
10, 11, 14, 47, 60, 83, 84
Cleanliness 39
Colour 29, 104
Commerce 50
Commodities 12, 50, 59, 70, 75,
77, 78, 89, 101, 114, 119, 120,
128, 134, 148
Communism x, 151

177

— communist(s) x, 38
— Stalinist communism xi, 8
Communitarian Socialists 71
Community spirit xiii, 11, 55, 74,
    113, 143, 146
Compartmentalisation 91
Compulsions xvii, 5, 6, 18
— compulsions of ruthless
    competition 7, 78
— self-destructive compulsion 6,
    17, 24
— suicidal compulsion 6
Computers 11, 12, 46, 63, 64, 71,
    72, 117, 132, 133
Conscience 22
Consumerism 16, 76, 131, 133,
    151
— consumerist 23, 133
Co-operative design centres 78
Corbusier, Le 97
Corporations xvi, 49, 74, 75, 120,
    131, 137, 138, 140. 143, 144
Cortex xvi, 18, 34, 56, 70, 109
— frontal lobes 9, 18, 48, 70
Cosmology 81
Cottrell, Theresa A. 19, 20, 21–22,
    23, 166
Crime xvi, 11, 62, 63, 64, 92,
    134, 135
Culture xiv, xviii, 9, 18, 27, 28,
    40, 41, 43, 44, 45, 50, 51, 56,
    57, 60, 66, 73, 79, 82, 83, 102,
    103, 114, 115, 117, 152
— acquisitive culture 114, 115,
    116
— consumer culture 16, 76, 133
— evolution of cultures xiv, 86
— psychotic cultures 7
— religious cultures 7, 152
— subculture 36
Czarism 166
— feudalism 166

D
Darwin, Charles 87
— Darwinian law 53, 55, 62, 91
Death 17, 164
Deconstructionists xvi
Defence mechanism 6
Dehumanisation 59
Delinquency 45
Democracy 7, 8, 74, 77, 84, 85,
    99, 114, 116, 118, 127, 128,
    148, 150, 162, 163
— 'new democracy' 77
— 'Rights of Man' 7
— social democracy x, 119, 121,
    129, 163
Depression 6, 14, 17, 22, 23, 49,
    51
Deprivation 49, 135
Devil 81, 82
Discipline 42, 44, 79
Discrimination 14
Doxiadis, C. A. 95, 96
Drives 6, 17, 36, 42, 102, 159
— aggressive drives 5
— death drive 17, 18
— destructive drive 159, 160
— exploratory drive 109
— oral-aggressive drive 43
— pregenital drive 40
— primitive drives xvi, 9
— secondary drive 17–18
— sexual drive 32
Drugs 11, 15, 51, 151
Dumbing down xvii, 14, 117,
    168–169
Durkheim, Emile 112

E
Ecologist, The 137, 141, 142,
    144–147
Ecology 136–148, 161, 162
Economics 130, 134, 151, 158,
    162

178

Planet xvii, 17, 47, 65, 86, 91,
136, 140, 143, 160, 161, 162,
163
— as a spaceship 159
— open planet 136
Plato xi, 13, 83, 84, 85, 150, 157,
160, 161
Play 87
Pleasure 24–25, 32, 34, 35, 39
Plutocracy 118, 131
Polis 84, 150
Political correctness 14, 15
Politics x, xv, 28, 117, 149, 150,
156
Pope, Alexander 44
Popper, Karl 85
Post, Dr Jerrold M. 153, 154, 155,
156
Poverty xii, 107, 136, 139, 159
Power xiii, 13, 18, 60, 98, 99,
105, 106, 117, 141, 152, 156
Preconscious 49
Pre-ego stage 26
Pregnancy 19
Prehistory xiv
Prejudice xi, xii, xvii, 13, 14, 44,
150
Priests 38, 39, 80
Primacies 32, 33, 34, 39, 40, 41,
42
Production 11, 37, 46, 59, 69, 70,
71, 73, 74, 77, 86, 120, 122,
137, 138, 149
— communal production 134,
161
Products 37, 59, 64, 70, 74, 76,
77
— invisible product 64
Profit xvi, 50, 59, 62, 63, 70, 73,
74, 76, 101, 118, 120, 127, 131,
132, 133, 134, 138, 146, 148
— profit motive 62, 70, 101, 119,
120, 131, 133, 138

Projection 14, 34, 35, 39
— self-projection 33, 35
Proletariat x, 107, 139
— 'new proletariat' 139
Protagoras 150
Psyche xvi, 18, 152
— collective psyche xiv, 7, 18
— psychic activities 102
— psychic apparatus 39
Psychiatrists 117, 133, 153
Psychoanalysis ix, xiii, xiv, xv, 32
— psychoanalysis of cultures 18
— psychoanalytic anthropology
18
Psychology 51, 154–156, 163
— political psychology 153
Psychological:
— psychological activity 34
— psychological differences 55
— psychological problems 35
— psychological stress 22
Psychopathology 11, 23
— psychopathology of a tyrant
153–156
Psychosis 7, 17, 96
— collective psychosis xvii, 7
— psychotic 6, 42, 156
— psychotic symptoms 7
— social psychosis 17, 25
Psychosomatic 19, 94, 104
Psychosphere 93
Psychotherapy xv, 17
Puberty 40, 48
— first puberty 41, 87
Public sector 123, 124
Puritan 97
Purpose 48, 55, 56, 57, 58, 70,
74, 75, 76, 77, 82, 84, 85, 86,
91, 115, 131, 134, 135
— universal purpose 159
Pyramids 106